If I Had Wanted a Trip
Throu
I Would Have Bought
My Own Ticket

Christine Pechacek

These pages contain my remembrances alone. They are my history. Our lives are never single events. It cannot be said that one life is independent or stands aloof from those who flow into and then out of a person's existence. I have written but a brief snapshot of the person I am and the influences that shaped my future. Due diligence has been taken to be as accurate as possible with regard to names and places.

ACKNOWLEDGEMENTS

I am grateful to my siblings for the memories they shared and the ones they helped me remember. My children remain two of my biggest fans and their encouragement is something I treasure. You are both loved beyond measure. Thank you to my beautiful daughter-in-law for asking me when I would write the next chapter of my life. To my oldest granddaughter who loved the title best of all, thank you. Thank you to all my grandchildren. You make me want to leave a legacy.

To my friend, Linda Stephison, who told me it was time to birth this baby. To Dennis Ginnard for his suggestions. To Chris Kliewoneit for helping me through the labyrinth of computer speak. Your patience is remarkable. Thanks beyond measure to Mary Jane Ogg for wading through that first draft. To Christine Anthony, photographer extraordinaire.

The deepest thanks to my husband, Daniel, for believing this was in me all along.

For Daniel Joseph Pechacek
We have each other.

AUTHOR'S NOTE

Growing up I did not wonder about my life. I did not ask why, what if, where I came from, or what did my future hold. This kind of introspection did not enter my thinking as I grew from childhood into adulthood. My days were spent zigzagging a course that kept me clear of the chaos that surrounded me every day of my young life. Finding ways to dodge bullets of rage fired randomly in our house was all consuming. My parents, swallowed up by their own misery, offered no oasis of comfort or sanity.

As an adult the questions began screaming for answers. The screams echoed in idiotic life decisions, fears of the unknown, stupid relationship choices, guilt, self-recriminations and just plain being pissed off about too many things.

I learned some things and sought answers to others along the way. The answers do not change anything but the gaps are filled with something more solid, and I can put faces on the good, the funny and the evil. I want my children and my grandchildren to know about me, who I was then, and who I am now. They deserve a history of the lives to which they are inextricably linked. But perhaps the best reason for wanting to leave to my children and grandchildren a history of my life was said to me by my sister.

"Hey Shirl, I'm going to write about our lives growing up," I said. "We have nothing, only bits and pieces of memories. Between the four of us," I added, "we can barely remember one complete life. I want more for my children and grandchildren. I want them to know about me, who I am and why."

"Good," Shirley said, "I want my grandkids to know why I'm crazy."

PROLOGUE

You can't cast a play in Hell and expect to have angels as actors.
Bobbi Billard

My family was poor. I knew it, my siblings knew it and my parents knew it. We were not distinguished from most of the other neighborhood families because they were poor as well. We were not poor in the "We may not have many material things but we have each other" sense. Our poverty reached down to suck in every aspect of our humanity. It enveloped us emotionally, physically and spiritually. It surrounded us and eventually swallowed our lives into a swamp of desperation. What grew from the putrid vapor were anger, despair, abuse, distrust, and ultimately our destruction. But it did not begin with our little family. It began much earlier.

JOSEPH

Joseph, My Father

My father, Joseph, grew up the middle child of five, and the only surviving male child born to Peter and Helen Wener. One brother died at age two from the Spanish influenza that ravaged the country around 1917. Another male child died at birth and a third before reaching the age of two. Along the way, four girls were born, putting my father in the middle. My Grandmother, Helen, became a widow too soon with five children to feed and no means of support.

Grandma Helen was a cruel and vicious mother. While none of the five Wener siblings escaped her abuse, my father was her unrelenting target. Helen did not become abusive following the death of her husband, and so it could not have been said the grief, stress and anguish of her life caused her to change. She was, at her core, a cruel and hateful woman. From this, my father grew to be a man.

As children my siblings and I had little contact with Grandma Helen. She lived alone in a tiny Airstream trailer in Detroit. Our occasional visits there with my father were quick and filled with angst. Mother and son spoke rapid-fire German and always in raised voices. She was old, wrinkled and bent with age. Her once red hair, now gray, was forever coiled atop her head and under a hairnet. The air in her tiny trailer was thick with the smell of kerosene and fried donuts. The donuts were always a treat. Each time as we left, my grandmother would slip us a dollar and whisper in our ears to hide it. My father, wise to her game, took the dollar and put it back on her tiny counter. What inevitably followed was a spirited exchange in German between my father and grandmother, ending with all of us getting in the car and leaving without the dollars.

SHIRLEY

My mother, Shirley, grew up in a home where money was in small measure more abundant. This did nothing to moderate the atmosphere of the home created by the monsters calling them-selves her parents. The eldest of three, Shirley was the only female. My Grandmother Marie did not punch, beat, kick, or scream vile things at my mother as Helen had done to my father. Marie's depth of evil was more insidious, reaching beyond beat-ings. Marie sat back with delib-erate blind eyes to my mother's

My Mother, Shirley

suffering as my grandfather, Art, repeatedly during my mother's youth, used her for his own sick pleasures. Her innocence was sto-len early by the pedophile who called himself her father.

Art and Marie lived close by in a tiny white asbestos-sided house that was once a garage. It sat on multiple acres along with sev-eral sheds of various sizes. If my grandfather worked at anything or somewhere, I was not aware of it. My Grandmother Marie had what was to me a frozen expression of anger on her face. Tight lipped with a perpetual scowl, I did not like her.

Grandma Marie was a chain smoker when smoking was fash-ionable. I was mesmerized by her smoking skills. Her cigarettes of choice were filtered Tarrytons. She would draw deeply on the cigarette and then as the smoke slowly came out her mouth, she drew it up her nose. The smoke never escaped but went up in a thick stream to her nostrils. This fascinated me and was some-thing I wanted to do when I grew up. Thankfully, as cool as I thought the smoke up your nose thing was, it remained a goal left unaccomplished.

JOSEPH AND SHIRLEY

From these grim beginnings, Joe and Shirley met and fell in love. They married and produced four children. The eldest, Nicholas, born in 1945, bore the name of one of my father's deceased brothers. At three years of age, Nicholas welcomed a sister, Christine. I had entered the family. When I was four years old, cute and blond, my baby sister came on the scene. Shirley Ann, named after my mother and forevermore called by her first and middle name together, was tiny, sweet, and adorable. She had big, round blue eyes that seemed to take in everything around her and dark, curly hair that framed her face. And last, but not least in 1958, Michael was born into the family.

My father, a carpenter by trade, built our home when Nick and I were very young and before Shirley Ann was born. The tiny house, set on three acres of land, had one bedroom, a living room, kitchen, an attic, and a small utility room, but no bathroom. This modern luxury came later. The bathroom must have been put in while I was still in diapers because I have no memory of a smelly outhouse or sitting in an outdoor structure on a wooden plank with a hole on the middle.

By outward appearances we were welcomed children and my parents were happy in their family life. Perhaps that is so, but a happy family life is not how I remember my childhood.

I cannot recall when, nor am I able to identify, the first bolt of thunder unleashed in our family. In its own twisted, psychotic way poverty with its day to day struggle for survival may have been the catalyst. My childhood memories are twists and turns in a dark, foreboding place where fear went to bed with you and dread greeted you each morning. My father's fits of rage began to be regular but not predictable. As children we knew he would explode, but just not when or why. Like a hand-grenade with the pin missing, his temper exploded and we, the tiny, frightened mice, ran for cover. Terrified that one of us had somehow, unknowingly set off the latest firestorm, we huddled as far out of sight as possible. Regardless of the supposed reason, his rage needed to be spent somewhere.

Joseph and Shirley, 1942

Nicholas, as the eldest, bore the brunt of the senseless cruelty that was always simmering under the surface of my father's soul. And so, like his mother before him, Joseph unleashed a torrent of cruel physical fury on my innocent brother. My first recollections of it are remote and blurred in my memory. At times, I think that I want to remember. I think that I must remember in order to make my past complete. My mind wants to close the gaps, straighten the crooked places so all the jagged pieces will fit together. But then, the gatekeeper in my head just slams shut those places of pain.

What I do remember are times of hiding from my father's fury and seeing my helpless brother attempt to ward off the blows. Clenching my fists and biting whatever was at hand, I screamed silently for my father's fury to stop. It never worked.

My mother, as powerless as we, stood helpless against the venting of his rage. She had had her humanity flayed from her heart and soul by the son of a bitch who wore the mask of father. My mother and father were two wounded, scarred people calling themselves parents, trapped in a prison of no escape. Unfortunately, four children had entered into their private hell. Silenced by fear, treading carefully in a house full of landmines, we carried on a daily existence well hidden from the prying eyes of the outside world. It was a time when, even if someone knew the unhappiness and sorrow in your home, it was not their business to speak of it or to acknowledge its existence. It was, after all, the 1950s and family was family. It was an age of innocence that venerated ideal family life.

Living on Frazho Road with all my friends was my escape hatch. It provided a world for me that did not exist inside my home where it was always dark and threatening. In the house we were not safe. It was a dangerous place for children to live and grow; but outside we ran, played, laughed, learned from each other and kept busy being kids. I loved it. Outside we ran the streets until dark, went to our friends without constant monitoring, played in ditches, rode bikes without helmets, and more often than not, no shoes, built bonfires at night and chased ice cream trucks. In the outside world I was safe and happy. In my home the walls closed in on me and it was the scariest place to be.

CHAPTER ONE

Growing up a baby boomer, I spent my early childhood in the 1950s. It was the decade of innocence, of the grandfatherly President Dwight D Eisenhower, of eating lunch with Soupy Sales, Saturday matinees at the Roseville Theater with what seemed like a thousand other screaming kids, and living in fear of the A-Bomb falling directly on our house at any moment. We did not have the recommended concrete bomb shelter fully equipped with enough food and water for the prescribed recovery time. This was a constant worry for me. My fear of being melted into a mass of slime by radiation fall-out was reinforced at school.

At regularly scheduled times throughout the school year my elementary school had bomb drills. They were much like fire drills only for bombs. The bell would ring, signaling all classrooms to go out into the hallway. Once in the hallway we sat on the floor up against the wall with our knees brought close to the chest, arms wrapped around our knees and head bent forward. We sat in our positions until the all-clear bell rang. This was to protect us from falling debris should the bomb drop near, or on the school. I was not convinced this was an effective plan but since there was no concrete bomb shelter at Alwood Elementary School, it was the best solution.

We lived in a lower middle-class neighborhood, with blue collar working dads, stay at home moms and dirt roads lined with houses, some new, but all plain and in various stages of disrepair. But they were also houses full of other kids, most of whom were my friends or my siblings' friends.

Life was all about playing. We played outdoors all the time, weather be damned. Summer, fall, winter and spring. Every season had some perfect thing to do outdoors. Every activity involved friends and our limitless imagination. We took pretending to a new level. No one had gadgets to occupy their time. The county ditch was near our house and a favorite gathering place. Boys hunted frogs, occasionally spearing a fat one, but mostly just catching and holding them. I do not recall ever hunting frogs. They were green, ugly and slimy. The ugly frog sport never caught on with me and my friends. We often preferred the game of travel.

In our driveway, my father had, for some reason, stored a rusted out Jeep with no roof and ripped seat covers. But it did have a steering wheel, gear shift on the column, and floor pedals that worked lickety-split. And because the Jeep was in my yard, I was the sole driver. We traveled to faraway places in that dilapidated vehicle, often stopping for gas or refreshments along the way.

My first grade teacher, Mrs. Allen, also lived on Frazho Road. I was awed by the fact that Mrs. Allen lived outside the classroom in a house and had a daughter Patty. I am sure there was a husband as well, but my amazement over the house and daughter thing stalled me from thinking she might actually be married like my own parents. It was too much.

One summer I became friends with Patty. She invited me over to her house to play and we spent the afternoon playing dolls in her bedroom. Patty was fun to be around and she had numerous toys, dolls, and games, all of which were in short supply at my house. Our friendship only survived one summer. Mrs. Allen's presence made me nervous and uncomfortable. We may have been playing dolls in Patty's very nice bedroom, but I still felt like I was in school every time her mother came around. She had that stern teacher look and I was certain she thought I was up to something that I should not have been. Patty did not have many friends in the neighborhood.

Mrs. Weidyke lived across the street from our house. A small, stooped over, wrinkled woman, she took in ironing. Women dropped off baskets of clothes one day and picked them up the next, ironed and folded, all for $5.00 a basket. She ironed seven days a week, all day. I believe she had several children but I cannot be certain.

Other neighbors, Mr. and Mrs. Beltowski had several children, four sons and one daughter. Mrs. Beltowski was kind to neighborhood kids, but she could yell. When she stood on her porch to summon her brood home, the air vibrated like thunder. They all ran home at the first call. The entire Beltowski clan was loud, rambunctious and fun to be around. Danny Pechacek, a neighbor and my brother's friend, told of the time he was invited to dinner at the Beltowski home. Mrs. B, as she was affectionately known, made a pot of chicken soup and when she served it up, the claws and beak were in it. Danny swore this was true. I did not witness it myself so I cannot say for certain.

The antithesis of the Beltowski family lived next door to us. The Dupuie family consisted of mom, a quiet woman, dad, who kept a tidy lawn, and two daughters, both older than my circle of friends. We never invited either of them to play in the ditch with us after a great rainfall. Both daughters always dressed in what we considered school clothes and never played outdoors. One of my earliest memories is sitting on Mr. D's front porch and talking to him in long streams of consciousness. He seemed to pay close attention and ponder my deep thoughts as he raked his lawn. He was a very nice man.

Directly across from our house lived Mr. and Mrs. Stahl. They had two sons. The Stahls' yard was surrounded by the only chain-link fence in the neighborhood. No one had fences on Frazho Road, not even the quiet Dupuie family with the immaculate lawn. Our neighborhood was a poor one and fences were a luxury not many could afford. As children running everywhere we went, fences would have made it difficult to run through the yards on the way to a friend's house. But a fence was necessary for the Stahls because they also had a dog, a Great Dane. That dog terrified me because it stood eye to eye with me whenever I came remotely close to the fence, which I diligently avoided. I was thankful that Mr. and Mrs. Stahl had a fence and equally pleased that they did not have any daughters who would have been my friends. I do not think I could have gotten past that giant dog thing even for another friend.

Behind our house was a field with a well-worn path marking the trail to the Thomas'. Barbara and J.J. Thomas were the neighbors with a Southern accent. They had three children, Bonnie, Cheryl, and a son Robbie, in that order. Barbara, a beautiful Southern belle, feminine and saucy, was my favorite. I loved her. She had long hair and wore it big and a little wild. The oldest daughter, Bonnie, was three years my senior and a friend of Janet Pechacek, another neighbor. Janet and Bonnie sometimes let me tag along with them, but I had to be seen and not heard. I went to the Thomas house as often as I could, trekking the field trail to their back door.

Barbara Thomas made iced coffee in the summer time. It was a delicious concoction with lots of milk, ice and loads of sugar. She served it in tall glasses packed with ice cubes. I was not allowed coffee at home but since this was cold and not hot, I set my mind that it was permissible.

Across the street and several houses down lived relatives on my mother's side. First, Aunt Stella and Uncle Gene, brother to my Grandfather Art. Their only son was killed in an Air Force training flight. After that, they rarely left their house. Uncle Gene was a selfish, abusive husband and a hoarder before hoarding was in vogue. Aunt Stella attempted suicide once but did not succeed. For the rest of her life she lived silently with a man who denied her basic human kindness and afforded her little more than the minimum of food and shelter. Aunt Stella eventually passed away with little to her name other than a couple of cotton house dresses and old shoes. Following Uncle Gene's death several years later, family members clearing out his house found rooms stacked from floor to ceiling with papers, new clothing, unworn shoes, and furniture. They also found $10,000 in cash in a paper bag under a couch cushion. When his will was read, family members learned he had left his estate of nearly $500,000 to a lady friend, specifically omitting family members.

Not far from this aunt and uncle lived my Great-Grandmother Zelke, who was the oldest person I had ever known, and one of the kindest. She would sit on her small sun porch and quietly rock back and forth in her glider, not talking, just smiling. I would sometimes sit with her on sunny days and also not talk. We both just glided back and forth. We never had a real conversation that I can remember. We would sit together in her glider in the warm sun that shown through the windows of the glassed-in sun porch. Sometimes I would ask for a glass of water because I liked the way her well water was frizzy and tickled my nose. She always poured it into a cobalt blue glass, and I liked that too. I really did love my Great-Grandmother Zelke. She died while I was still very young.

Finally, there were my maternal grandparents who lived between my aunt and uncle, who I never saw, and my Great-Grandmother Zelke. They were sneaky, unkind people who hated my father and consequently, showed little regard for me and my siblings. This fact was not discussed but was nonetheless evident. Small children are sometimes very wise. We are silent in the face of ill treatment, having been taught to be quiet and respectful around adults, even stupid and cruel ones. We never spoke as we watched our cousins open more and better gifts at Christmas. No one pointed out that Grandma Marie and Grandpa Art ignored our birthdays and in general ignored us.

Of the two, Art did favor children with his attention occasionally. Done in dark places, it was the kind that came with threats made to ensure the dirty secret. A true bastard, Art remained so until his death. He was the kind of evil you feared most and felt powerless to escape. I avoided them both as much as possible.

Marie is long dead, as is Art. And while I refrained from dancing on the dirt now shoveled and packed down on top of them, neither did I shed a tear or feel one second of emotion resembling sadness or loss.

CHAPTER TWO

Pechacek. What kind of name was that? Who could even spell that name? Well, whatever kind of name it was, a whole family of them had moved in next door to our small house. At five years old, it was the first new house I had ever seen. This house was not old and worn like the rest of the houses in the neighborhood. It had been build right before our eyes. My brother and I had seen the men come day after day to put it up piece by piece. We had watched as men came with huge trucks and poured concrete for a front porch with a sidewalk leading all the way to the driveway. Having a concrete walk all your own made this family pretty uppity to our way of thinking.

Then one day after the house was finished, the family came; father, mother and three children. As kids, all we cared about were new kids coming to live in the neighborhood. How many boys and how many girls. And we wanted to know what kind of things they did for fun. We had our own list of fun things, which remained sacrosanct and well-guarded. The neighborhood talk was that this family of Pechaceks came from a place in Detroit called "The Projects." That alone made them strange and a little dangerous.

My brother, Nicky, and I stayed aloof for a few days and did not rush to judgment. The neighborhood hierarchy was already set as far as we were concerned. Nicky and I knew our place. We decided to stand our ground against any challengers. At five years old, I was as close to the bottom of the rung as I wanted to be. We circled our wagons and waited.

Nicky, eight years old, and I stood on the tiny blob of concrete that served as our porch and watched the new people next door. We did not wave or smile. Standing straight and tall with arms hanging at our sides, we watched. As always, I carefully eyed my big brother for what to do next. Nicky stood silent and stared, which is what I did as well. Our careful observations noted three children.

Danny, 1952

Danny, eldest and only boy came in at ten years old. He was big, with dark brown hair, brown eyes and walked with the bravado of a new kid entering territory that just might be dangerous. We learned his name when his mother called for him throughout the day. Her face appeared and a high pitch scream followed, "DANNY!" It was like nails on a chalkboard.

Her shrill call did not seem to bother Danny. He would momentarily pause in whatever at that moment required his attention, but did not move towards his mother's call. He seemed to weigh whether or not the summons was worthy of interruption. After contemplating long enough to require a second nail on the chalkboard call, he headed to the door. We reasoned that Danny must be one tough kid. It was probably from living in The Projects.

Next in line, Janet, slightly younger at eight years old, was tall, at least she appeared tall to my smaller frame. She had light brown hair and was on the chubby side. I mention that only because the neighborhood did not see many chubby kids, and it made for a point of interest. Not only had this family moved to our neighborhood from a strange, unknown place called The Projects but their appearance was also different. Maybe all project kids looked the same. We reserved judgment on that point as well.

Rounding out the Pechacek kids at eighteen months old was Teresa. There's not much you can tell about a baby. We ignored her just as we ignored Shirley Ann, our own baby sister of the same age. We took little note of the parents, Joe and Milly. As far as we knew, moms stayed in the house all day doing things they called work, except on Mondays when they came outside to hang laundry. And as far as dads went, they left every day to go someplace to get money so moms could buy groceries. It was all rather boring to us.

But this Pechacek dad also did something we had never seen, but had heard whispered. He did not just ride motorcycles—big ones—but he rode with a gang. The gang wore black leather jackets and strange black leather hats. We wondered if these men might be criminals. They might even be dangerous. But gradually we got bored with that possibility. As far as we could tell, the gang consisted of a bunch of regular men who did lots of talking and examining motorcycles. Occasionally a bushel basket of parts went into a work shed and days later out came a motorcycle. While such things might be a curiosity, it soon became just another thing about the Pechaceks that we ignored unless it directly involved one of us, like getting a ride on one of the motorcycles.

Watching the motorcycles come and go on the weekends made it look exciting. I wanted to take a ride on one but never spoke up. Such boldness was beyond me. But I often casually stood around, ready to jump at the chance should anyone offer. One afternoon, I was specifically invited for a ride. I nearly shook with anticipation and fear. I ran home, got a jacket and ran back to await my turn. The day wore on and I was forgotten. It never occurred to me to speak up and remind someone that I was still waiting for the promised ride. Even as young as I was, keeping quiet and never speaking out to any adult was already ingrained in me. Instead, I went home in tears, disappointed.

Despite the new neighbors and their seemingly former wild life in the Projects, our lives settled into the sameness of every day routines. We went to school, came home, played outside, ate dinner, and went back outside to play until the first street lights signaled us home. We never considered that our lives might be simple to the point of boring.

The Pechaceks had assimilated nicely. Janet occasionally invited me over to play dolls. That was fun mainly due to the fact that she had really cool dolls and doll clothes. My dolls were all hand-me-downs and appeared in clothes eked out of things found around the house. My brother, Nicky, and Danny had become friends and Shirley Ann and Teresa were playing together as much as 18 month old babies can manage to do. The two families, the Pechaceks and the Weners appeared to have developed close friendships among all family members. That is how it appeared to the outside world. Inside our world, it was a very different story.

My parents lived an already fragile existence, each day teetering on chaos with rage simmering relentlessly and too often erupting without warning. Our seemingly normal lives were like a boil, swollen red, puss filled and hot, ready for the one prick that would burst the carefully guarded core to expose the nasty infection.

Unfortunately for all of us, the point of the needle came in the form of our next door neighbors. It became apparent early on that Joe, next door Joe, and my father, also Joe, were not destined to be buddies, friends, or chums. As different as apples are from broccoli, Joe and Joe possessed nothing in common other than a name happened on them at birth. Milly and Shirley became friends. Milly was friendly however, in as much as it gave her access to my father. That became apparent early on and advanced quickly. Like a beam of radar, Milly's sights were set. As a young girl, I noticed her presence at our house frequently, just chatting and drinking coffee. Milly and my mother could often be found sitting around our kitchen table in friendly conversation. Then my father joined them. Soon my mother was absent from this new friendship, working evenings at a local grocery store to put food on our table in hard times.

The chats and cups of coffee lingered longer and became more frequent between my father and Milly. Next door Joe was not in sight. Always smiling and friendly, Milly stealthily optimized her position in the neighborhood and in our home to her advantage. Certainly my mother's absence made it convenient for my father to engage in this in friendship, soon to become infidelity. The mask of friendship remained in place. Before long trips together were planned. Joe, Shirley, and their children, Milly and her children, all traveled north for a day or two to spend at our small cabin at Shay Lake. We must have appeared to be a happy little group, Joe and his harem. Nothing was farther from the truth.

In retrospect, I choose to believe that my father's guilt drove his anger to a new level and intensity. As his family, we could do nothing right. Increasingly morose and silent in our presence, he became jovial and charming each time Milly appeared. My brother and I sat in our small living room and watched the animated conversations taking place. My father's laugh was deep and low as he leaned in close to Milly, hanging on her every word. And she obviously found my father fascinating as well. At times, their voices became whispers, eyes locked on each other. I did not understand what it meant, but I did not like it. I was left out of something I did not understand. We were all being left behind.

I cannot remember my mother being a part of this new period in my father's life. Some important dynamic of our young lives was changing. I could not name it, I dared not question what it was, but it was real, palpable, and to a young child, did not feel right. More than my mother's physical presence was fading. Her standing as wife and mother was threatened by this evil slithering silently around her home and all that she held precious, all that was rightfully hers. It was as though she sat outside our circle now, in some unnamed and dark place.

If my mother fought against this encroaching danger, I cannot say. Perhaps the increased fighting and screaming we heard in the dead of night were last ditch efforts to ward off an enemy she was not equipped to face alone. My father became a full blown Dr. Jekyll and Mr. Hyde. Our house, once rumbling with fear and deceit, now exploded with fury and treachery, sending my brother and me to hide from the shrapnel. As innocent victims of this downfall, we became clay in the hands of the evil potter. This potter was busy forming and shaping patterns in our young lives which were to become grim realities as we grew to adulthood.

CHAPTER THREE

My mother was a hardworking, beautiful woman who took pride in what she did for her family. That pride showed in a clean house, starched, ironed clothing, and delightful smells emanating from our kitchen. She was sometimes quiet, seldom stern, and had a laugh that lit up a room. If I reach back, I can remember her as a happy woman, doing what made her happiest, caring for all of us. Not so deeply buried, however, are the memories of the time when the dark slipped over her soul and she became sad and withdrawn, battered by the same life she once loved.

Being a housewife in the 1950s meant that laundry day was done on one specific day of each week, and on Frazho Road in Warren, Michigan, that day was Monday. Although my mother never left the house on Mondays, visited with neighbors or sat to idle the day away, she never missed any neighborhood events. That was because each and every other wife and mom was engaged in the same task on the same day, laundry. It seemed that Mondays had, in an ancient rite of past civilizations, been deemed the day of the wash, _so shall it be!_

Laundry was not merely a chore drudgingly done on the fly, casually sandwiched in between other household chores. Laundry at 14800 Frazho Road was the main event each and every Monday beginning early and continuing throughout the entire day. The smell of hot water mixed with TIDE laundry soap and bleach wafted its way from the back room of our house to make its way up the rough, unpainted, wooden stairs to our attic bedrooms. The smell of laundry day hung heavy in our windowless, hot bedrooms.

Although we all referred to the tiny spaces at the top of the stairs as bedrooms, it was the attic and never became anything else. The sloped roof never became a ceiling. The attic never saw paint. Turning over in our tiny beds as we slept often resulted in becoming nudged up against the sloping roof. Doing so too swiftly resulted in raw skin on your nose and even the occasional splinter. The small space had two beds. I slept in one and my sister, Shirley Ann, four years my junior, slept in the other. Nick, as the eldest had the unfortunate privilege to have his own room. At the end of the attic, his space was even smaller. The meager air circulation never made its way back into the tiny space where he slept. He seemed to manage, although the lack of air may have contributed to his sour attitude much of the time.

One by one with Nicky being the last to wake up, we made our way to the back room to watch as mom did the laundry. The laundry room was compact with one window and a back door. The space held a tall cabinet, which housed laundry necessities. TIDE, bleach, starch, one iron, extra clothespins, and a few hangars were always on hand. A wringer washer sat pushed against the wall until Monday mornings when it was rolled out to the middle of the room for easy access and ease of movement for my mother. In the corner of the cramped room was the deep sink used as a receptacle for dirty wash water once a cycle was complete. The giant hose was connected to the hot water faucet and filling the giant tub began.

The dirty laundry, separated into piles according to colors, went into the large tub. The glub-swish sound signaled that the clothes were being tossed, turned and flip-flopped in the soapy water. My mother stood vigil over the tub occasionally using a broom handle to separate tangled garments. After several minutes the wringer housed above, and connected to the washtub was turned on. Carefully my mother scooped out a garment and put

14

its edge close to the two rollers. Dirty, soapy water was squeezed out and fell back into the washtub. Once every piece of laundry in the load had passed through the wringing process, the entire mound lay in the large wicker basket at my mother's feet. Up to three loads might be washed in the same water unless it appeared too dark and mucky. If so, the process of emptying dirty water and refilling with clean began. Finally all the washed laundry was put through a clean water rinse. It was exhausting for my mother and consumed her every Monday.

The clothes dryer consisted of two steel poles firmly planted in concrete in the backyard. Each pole, approximately six feet high, held six hooks spanning the crossbar, to which a rope clothesline was strung to form six taught lines. Hanging from one line was a cloth bag with wire in the top seams.

Inside the bag were two kinds of wooden clothespins some good and some evil. For me, inanimate objects had personalities. Some were good and others were evil. My judgment as to which was arbitrary. And since I kept this particular power of mine to make the distinction a secret, it was never questioned. This, of course, made me correct each time. One type of clothespin was squeezed together at its top, hooked on the line atop the corners of cloth pinching items firmly in place. The others were straight smooth ones that looked like tiny fence posts and a groove that pushed down to hold the clothes on the line. I preferred the tiny fence posts. They were sophisticated in their smooth lines and rounded head and, as a result, were good. The squeeze kind were crisscrossed, out of line, and had wires holding them together with a tiny gear. This formation made them bad and therefore stupid. Clothes hung on our line every week, year round. In Michigan winters that meant frozen sheets. The sight of sheets freezing on clotheslines was a normal winter sight.

Another laundry day staple was the ironing board and heavy iron. Collars, cuffs, ruffles on dresses and the ever present cro-cheted doily were carefully dipped in a small bucket of starch mixed with hot water, then left to dry to become weird, twisted shapes. Clothes slated to be ironed, which was almost every item washed, were first dried outside on the line and then dampened prior to ironing. It seemed to me a strange thing to do, wash and dry the clothes only to get them wet again—on purpose.

For this process an empty Pepsi bottle was filled with water and capped with a cork which held a tiny colander like top. Laying out each item my mother shook the Pepsi bottle full of water over the entire piece. The item was carefully rolled up in a neat roll to be pushed down into a large plastic bag until it was filled with other dampened items. The bag was left for a day or two to ensure each item was evenly dampened. The timing was essential. Left too long meant the clothes might mildew, either requiring re-washing or being ruined with black splotches of mildew scattered over the piece. My mother apparently had a secret timer in her head that allowed her to discern when the bag was ready. One by one the items were brought out, ironed and made to look brand new.

One last item in the small space was my mother's prized Mangle. To my recollection, ours was the only house to have such a superb piece of laundry equipment. Fashioned after a cleaners' press, my mother sat to iron sheets, pillow cases, my father's occasional dress shirt, our dresses and any other pieces she could work around the strange press.

The large cylinder was covered in soft cotton. It was heated until hot steam rose from the cotton covering. Sitting on a small wooden stool, she pulled down the long handle and held it until a burst of steam rose. We had been warned never to touch this item as it was highly dangerous and severe consequences would result. My mother related horrific stories of young children having the skin cooked right down to the bone on hands and arms because they disobeyed this order. I was convinced this must be true; however, it did not deter me from experimenting with the dangerous tool whenever possible.

Memories of laundry day with its routine, the smell of hot water and TIDE, and the moisture in the house left by load after load of wet laundry, remains a time of comfort for me. It reminds me when our house was a home, each of us with a role to play and happy to do so. It was a time when my mother was happy and content to be a wife, our mother, and a good friend to those around her. My mother smiled then and laughed with friends and family. She cooked and cleaned, keeping home and hearth together for the ones she loved so much, and the one at the top of her list was my father.

CHAPTER FOUR

My mother, Shirley, worked part-time at Sy's Grocery Market, a neighborhood store located just a few blocks from our house. She worked in the evenings, which meant she was gone most nights until 9:30 or later. She worked nights so that my brother and I never came home from school for lunch or after school to an empty house. This schedule also made it convenient for my father to openly carry on with his, by now, confirmed girlfriend of next door. His boldness in being a fraud of a husband, a bully of a father and gallant lover to his partner in adultery was exceeded only by his ability to blame my mother for all his troubles.

Our lives had settled into a quasi-twilight-zone home life. On any given night it was normal for my brother and me to see my father at our kitchen table, the light brown with gold flecks Formica table, enjoying lively, spirited conversations with Milly. She, for her part found his repartee witty and obviously enthralling as evidenced by the rapt attention she gave to his every word. For the occasional diversion, my father would sometimes impress Milly with his culinary skills.

My father was a pretty good cook. His offerings were limited but the ones he had mastered were delicious. One particular dish was so delectable; we lined up to get a taste. My mother did all her frying in black, cast iron pans. The frying pans came in various sizes with the largest one at ten inches in diameter and four inches deep. It was a monster and the most used fry pan in the kitchen. The cast iron pans had a special process for cleaning, which did not really consist of cleaning. After each use, the oil was dumped into an empty can, any food scraps stuck to the bottom scraped out and discarded. Finally, my mother would take a soapy dishrag and wipe the inside of the pan first and then the outside. This was repeated with a rinsed cloth. The pan was set on a hot burner for a minute or two to dry and then stored back in the oven. Over time, the oils were sealed inside making it a revered frying pan.

This was the pan my father used to cook, or fry to a crisp in hot oil, pork chops. The chops were always thin sliced, bone-in with plenty of fat left on. My father had a special affinity for meat fat. As a young boy one of the regular lunches he and his four sisters consumed were bacon grease sandwiches. My grandmother scavenged whatever she could to feed her children after my grandfather's early death. They seldom, if ever, had jelly, jam or preserves but there was bacon grease aplenty. Used for frying and preserved in a jar kept in the middle of the dining table for future use, it made for a filling sandwich. My father claimed to like it. He said it tasted sweet. I did not think that could possibly be true but accepted the statement as long as my father did not start thinking it would be good for us. He had some strange ideas about what was good for you.

More than one home remedy had been hoisted on our unsuspecting bodies. One of my father's favorites was eating Vick's Vapor Rub as a cure for sore throats, ear aches or things in between. For a sore throat my mother would rub generous amounts of the greasy substance from ear to ear, making certain to cover the entire throat and down onto the chest. Next a cloth, usually a clean rag of some sort, was wrapped around the throat and secured with a giant safety pin. The final touch was when my father held out the giant blue jar of Vick's. This signaled that you take a finger full and swallow the rancid mess. I can neither prove nor disprove its healing abilities. However, I suspect it speeded recovery only to avoid another swallow.

My father's method of frying pork chips was to plop the pork in enough hot oil to lube a small automobile. Salt and pepper were sprinkled on the meat and the frying began. Snaps, crackles, and sizzles flew up and out making a six foot radius a danger zone. My father did not believe in covering up hot crackling grease. You just stood back if you had any brains and if not, it was your own damn fault. My father must have somehow been immune to being burned by the hot grease because he kept a constant vigil at the stove, alternating between turning chops over and moving them around in the pan. Once fried to my father's satisfaction, the next step was removing the chops to a plate and setting the frying pan to a cool burner. This was our cue to line up.

I did not really care whether I actually ate a pork chop or not, but I always made certain I was second in line for the real treat. My father would have a stack of bread slices waiting on a plate. One at a time he dropped a slice into the grease, let it soak, turned it over to soak the other side and then handed one to Nicky. Next it was my turn. The taste was both sweet and juicy. I loved it. Lastly was Shirley Ann, who being the smallest and last in line ended up with the least amount of juice on her bread. That was too bad because it was delicious, but I did not share mine. Age had to have some privileges. I suppose this was not far from bacon grease sand-wiches. And if they were half as good as the pork chop bread, I was maybe willing to reconsider.

Another thing my father found delicious was what I called "gag in a glass." For some unexplained reason, probably related to bacon grease sandwich brain damage, my father also thought that raw eggs and bread were a delicacy. For this gourmet dish, he broke two or three eggs into a glass, beat them with a fork to mix yolk and whites thoroughly until it was one solid yellow mass resembling a disease in incubation. Then he dunked fresh white bread slices into the mixture and ate the bread pieces. RAW. It was more than I could bear to watch. I made a hasty exit whenever I saw the preparations begin. If I was gone, he could not offer me a taste. When my father offered you a taste of something, it was not only foolish to say no thanks, it could be dangerous.

"What the hell do you mean you don't like it? You don't even know that yet. Now shut up and get over here and try it. Damn it!"

We tried whatever was being forced upon us, accepting that we may die from the morsels that stared back, but believing that death was better than my father's wrath should we refuse. As a child I never experienced a middle ground with my father. It was his way or suffer the consequences.

The pork chops were a highlight but nothing compared to apple streusel, a pastry my father learned to make from his mother. Preparing this dish was not an idle pastime done on a whim. It was an event of mega proportions. The first thing my father did was peel and core apples and slice them into thin pieces. It required many apples, so big yellow was brought out of the cupboard. It was the largest in a set of bowls my mother used for mixing.

The set consisted of four bowls, graduated in size. Big Yellow was the largest; it looked big enough to put a baby in for a bath. The next was a red one, then green and finally the smallest, an orange one. For apple streusel my dad always used Big Yellow. The sliced apples along with the sugars and spices were mixed together and set aside. The real event took place on the kitchen table. My father cleared and wiped down the table and in the middle he dumped flour, sugar and a bit of salt. Next he made a sort of mountain of flour mixture, put a hole in it with two fingers, cracked in a couple of eggs, poured milk over top and added some unnamed fat. My father was obsessed with fat. This mess he mixed with his hands until it was gooey dough, dropped more flour on the table and kneaded the dough. Next, the rolling pin was brought out to roll and flatten, roll and flatten, roll and flatten until the dough nearly covered the table top. Still it was not thin enough. It had to be paper thin before it was streusel ready. He would slowly and carefully stretch the dough one inch at a time. In the process, there wear tears and holes which always brought verbal eruptions and a curse or two from my father. Finally, when this parchment like dough covered the entire table and even hung over the sides, it was ready for the apple mixture to be spread thinly over the dough's surface. The dough was then rolled up in one long tube, curled around to fit on the baking pan and put in the oven to bake. It smelled wonderful and tasted the best. We all hung around for this treat and needed no prodding to try it.

This production was of course performed for Milly . . . while my mother was gone. Working.

CHAPTER FIVE

By the time I was four years old, I had developed a stuttering problem. It was also when my bed-wetting phase began. Both the stuttering and the bed-wetting terrified me, not because at four or five years old I was capable of self-examination into the whys of my problems; but, I lived in fear of the consequences of such unacceptable acts. Both issues just pissed my father off.

As to the stuttering, I did not occasionally stumble over a word or merely have difficulty in bringing forth the word I wanted to say. Speaking a complete sentence was often beyond my scope. As a result, I remained as silent as possible on every occasion involving my father.

Children in our house practiced silence as a matter of course. Silence was not only golden for my brother and me; it was often a matter of survival. You did not question adults. Having an opinion was not possible. The only opinion in our house was my father's. It was more law than opinion. Nor were we allowed emotions in our house. My father's anger ruled us all and became the only emotion we recognized.

Me, Age 5

In fact, rage became the culture of our family. My father ruled by fear. Perhaps today he would be identified as a rage-aholic. I knew him as Daddy. First and foremost, my mother lived under his reign. She submitted in all ways. Having been brought up under the rule of a cruel, abusive mother, the sacrifice of a pedophile father, any vestige of self she may have at one time possessed was long gone. Life was rarely pleasant for my mother. That was a fact. There was no one to rescue my mother, and she was without armor in the almost daily battles against my father's rage. I never saw anyone rush to her aid or rise to defend her.

If my mother was not at hand, if on the days she worked outside the home for little pay and long hours, the eldest son stood in her stead. Small, sometimes frail, with dark hair, unlike my blond father, Nicky became the target. One afternoon in our small backyard, my brother and I worked diligently doing my father's bidding in the small garden behind our garage. My father fancied himself a farmer at heart. Having been given our orders for the assigned tasks, we both set to work. We neither spoke nor dared to question. There was no playful banter. My father commanded and we worked. Suddenly, in a breath, my father's fury exploded. Who knows what demons reared their ugly heads inciting him to strike. In truth, there were no reasons. I looked up and he was coming at my brother, my friend, my sibling, my sometimes protector, screaming words neither of us could understand. I stared, frozen with fear, deaf to anything other than the sound of my own heart pounding. My father had a garden rake in his hand. Blow after blow landed on my brother's back. Nicky was crying and desperately trying to escape. There was nowhere to go. To run from

26

my father only meant greater fury when he caught up with you. It was better to patiently endure, duck as much as possible, and try to avoid the blows. Even in my silence, I dared not think of how wrong and cruel my father was at that moment. My mind was frozen, unable to grasp an independent thought of injustice, of abuse, or how insane were our lives as children.

Then as quickly as it began, it was over. In its wake Nicky cried deep sobs, fear and sadness in his face. I ran to escape and huddled in a corner by the garage. My body shook uncontrollably. Physically running from chaos or conflict became a pattern in my life for many years. Raised voices sent me out of a room. Simmering unease drove me to leave whatever situation threatened to erupt. Any attempt at self-defense paralyzed me.

On that glorious, sunny day it was not the first burst of cruelty spent on an innocent victim in our house and it would not be the last. Nicky and I knew that. Our only defense was to hide as much as possible, be silent whenever possible, and struggle to think one step ahead. What did he want? What should we do or not do in every situation. My mode of operation was to be super-good daughter. Good grades. Excellent behavior at all times. Never disobey. Never try something new. Never venture into the unknown. Never risk venturing forth. Smile at all times. Make every effort to anticipate all things for all people. Above all, hide who you are or who you might become. The world, like home, must be dangerous.

One early morning, after my mother had left the house for parts unknown, probably to escape, the call came up the stairs to get up. Sleeping in was never an option for the Wener children. If my father was awake, the whole house was awake. My brother and I scurried down the stairs. There was no good morning to greet us. We sat at the kitchen table eating our breakfast. Already tense, my father was pacing back and forth in the kitchen, smoking a cigarette, coffee close at hand. He paused to look in a drawer for some object. It was not in the spot where he expected to find it. The fury that perpetually simmered so near the surface boiled over. The drawer came out in one vicious pull, scattering its contents across the kitchen floor. On a roll with this tantrum, his arm swept across the top of our refrigerator, resulting in every item that had set on its top flying across the floor to join the contents of the drawer. Further engaged by a mess of his own making, he screamed for my brother and me to "clean up that damn mess." Scurrying like mice in a cage with nowhere else to go, we ran to gather the items, find the right place for each, and put them all back.

In preparation for entering first grade at Alwood Elementary School, a new winter coat had been purchased for me. It was beautiful. I treasured my brand new coat. One evening my father's sister, Eva, came to visit. Once again my mother was not at home but Milly appeared in her place at our table, replacing my mother, both as wife and now as pseudo-sister-in-law.

As they talked, my father called to me from the kitchen, "Go get your new coat and show it to Aunt Eva."

I obeyed instantly. On this matter, I was a quick learner. Excited to show off my new coat, I ran and brought the soft, pretty grey coat into the kitchen. I stood silently and smiled, the coat held up as high as I could get it.

My father barked, "Well, tell her about it. Say something."

I jumped and began, knowing already what would come out. "T—T—Th—Th- This is m—m—m—my ne—ne—new coat." I was breathless with the effort to finish the sentence.

I heard a soft giggle from my Aunt. Milly stared and said nothing.

My father shouted, "Oh, just get out of here."

As I ran from the room, I heard the disgust in my father's voice, "I don't know why the hell she can't just talk without stuttering."

So deep seated was my fear, not even in my deepest thoughts did I dare speak a word against my father's unjust and cruel behavior in our home. I became incapable of identifying or organizing my own feelings and emotions. This set up a firm pattern for my life.

Anger I understood. It was the only emotion I recognized as valid. But anger was only acceptable if displayed by the man in charge of the house, first my father and then I transferred the same thought pattern to my husband. The sole reaction I knew in my life to injustice, to lies, to betrayal, to every attack against my personhood, to every thief that came to steel what was rightfully mine, was to remain silent. Denying the truth was paramount if addressing painful things meant I must come forward and speak for myself. Speaking up, expressing an opinion, or defending myself was forbidden. Anger would ensue. Better to be betrayed. Safer to suffer, to accept the lies and endure the pain. Safer to lose everything I held dear rather than to speak and be slapped.

CHAPTER SIX

The Roseville Theater was located on the corners of Gratiot Avenue and Utica Road, making it six miles from our house and out of my free roaming territory. At six years old, I was restricted to just two blocks from my front door. This rule was fine with me as all my friends up to that point lived within the two block territory. Mere physical distance did not deter our frequent visits to the Roseville Theater however. Each Saturday afternoon the theater was home to what looked to me like every kid in the cities of Warren, Roseville and Utica. The crowds began arriving close to noon. Car after car lined up, each one inching closer to the drop off spot, which was as close as possible to the ticket booth. Parents did not park. Instead cars came to a slow crawl, never completely stopping, as kid after kid opened a door, jumped out and never glanced back. There was always the fear that the one ahead of you might get the last ticket. It never happened but each Saturday was a nail bitter. The matinees meant two feature films, at least two cartoons, and previews of coming attractions. The ticket booth was on the outside of the theater, not inside away from the weather, which seemed to be rainy more often than not.

I was most definitely too young to be dropped off alone so my brother Nicky was in charge. At nine years old and three years my senior, he knew his way around the theater scene. Before leaving home, we were each given twenty-five cents for our ticket and another twenty cents apiece for candy to eat during the show. Being a man of the world, Nicky immediately took charge of our money for safe keeping.

One of my parents would drive Nicky and me to the spot where all the other kids stood screaming and milling about. Once out of the car and on the sidewalk, Nicky held my hand in a vise grip, which felt good to me. All I could see were backs, legs, arms, and heads. We stood in the long line, both of us timid and quiet, anxious to get our tickets.

Finally at the front of the line Nicky told the lady, "Two please," handed over the money he so carefully guarded and waited for the paper tickets. Tickets in hand, we went through large glass doors and stepped into another line. At the head of this line stood a man waiting to take the tickets we had just purchased. Tearing them in half, he put the halves into a tall spindle-like holder, which held the hundreds of other ticket halves. I was silent during the entire process, holding my big brother's hand in a grip that must have cut off circulation. He never chided me or pushed me away in impatience. He held tightly and carefully dragged me along behind him.

Next stop was the candy counter. My eyes reached mid-way on the glass, giving me a clear view of all the choices. Nicky's chin was at counter level so he did all the talking. He quickly asked me what I wanted and since this was a decision requiring careful forethought, I had pondered the delights the night before and was ready with my answer. Red licorice was most definitely one of my preferred choices. With the rest of the money, Nicky was able to buy several items. I considered him a very good bargain hunter. Candy in hand, we made our way into the theater to find a seat.

The movie had yet to begin so kids of all ages and sizes ran, shuffled through rows of seats, climbed over seats to get closer to friends and screamed for no apparent reason other than the fact that every other kid was doing the same. My brother found our seats. I left that important decision to his good judgment as well and to the fact that I could not see where I was going. The theater lights were still up but the running, shoving mass of kids kept me so off balance that it required holding Nicky's hand in the same iron grip. Besides, I knew where we would sit, the first or second row. It was where we always sat at the Saturday matinées.

Secure in our seats, Nicky took care of the next item on our weekly agenda; putting our storehouse of candy in our safe. Taking his light jacket off, my brother made a pouch of the jacket's back and then folded the sleeves over in front to make a cover. Inside went all our delectable sweets. Over the course of the afternoon, Nicky would check our supply, parcel out bits at a time, leaving the remaining delicacies for later. My brother was a master of the candy supply. Our Saturdays at the theater never differed in its routine but the movies did.

We watched Abbott and Costello's *40 Foot Bride of Candy Rock,* which seemed to me a plausible and interesting plot; *Abbott and Costello Meet Frankenstein,* and several other comedies. The horror genre followed and for this I blame most of my childhood fears.

First to come was *The Crab That Ate Chicago* or some similar grisly title. Evidently, a nuclear explosion caused little crabs on the beach to become as large as city houses and then the monster crabs set about to eat people and destroy the world. It was useless to point out to me that crabs are not flesh eaters or that anatomically crabs cannot become giants. I saw it with my own eyes on the big screen; therefore, it must be true.

Then one Saturday we sat and watched as a substance resembling green tapioca moved entirely of its own volition, selected victims and dissolved them in their beds as they slept unsuspectingly. *The Green Slime* movie, which was the actual title, caused me to sleep tucked up tightly in blankets fitted as snugly as possible over my body. The Slime's victims had carelessly slept with covers un-tucked and hanging over bedsides, leaving limbs exposed. This foolish move resulted in being dissolved. My brilliant precaution caused me on many nights to be near heat stroke in our hot, air-less attic bedroom. But I rested easier knowing I was protected against the Green Slime's vaporization of my body.

Nothing, however, prepared me for *The Creature From the Black Lagoon.* All the cinema- graphic touches were present in this production to make it a classic: a large monster swimming about in dark murky water, unsuspecting adults on a boat going about important business, usually government business, and one beautiful innocent woman who, not surprisingly, loved to take long swims alone in the dark murky waters of the Black Lagoon. In scene after scene, the beautiful woman swam, completely unaware while the creature lurked close enough to touch her, but of course did not. For the moment she was safe. A theater full of children screamed for her to be careful. Watch out! All of course to no avail. Eventually, she was in deadly peril but miraculously rescued by the handsome men on the boat. But not, it seems, before the creature had developed a little thing for this woman and so did not kill her. Finally, the poor creature was attacked by the men intent on protecting the alluring woman in the bathing suit. That movie ended forever my desire to swim in waters where the bottom was hidden from my clear view

From my initiation into the 1950s horror genre at the Roseville Theater, I felt I had graduated to being able to stay up on a Saturday night to watch SHOCK THEATER on our black and white television. My older brother had been afforded this dubious privilege already. The movie began at 11:30 p.m., an unheard of hour to be awake. It was the only night of the week when TV programing did not end at midnight. Each week featured a shocking horror film. My mother had been resolute in denying me this opportunity. But I was a master at wearing her down, having worked on it for many years already. And so finally, exhausted from my whining, begging and amazing logic, my mother relented.

The anticipated Saturday night arrived. At the appointed hour my brother and I sat down in front of our one and only television, a 12x12 inch screen housed in a box big enough to comfortably hold one or two good sized dogs. We never sat on furniture to view the television. It was much better appreciated sitting cross-legged on the floor a mere eighteen inches from the screen. My parents had gone to bed so there was no one to tell us to move back or we would go blind.

The typical horror music came forth as a prelude. The title appeared. There were no television guides that we knew of so programming was always a surprise to us. The feature this Saturday night was *Dracula,* starring Bela Lugosi. By movies' end, any sense of peace and safety I may have managed to retain in spite of green slime, giant crabs that ate people, and lagoon creatures was gone. I now faced a new challenge: how to protect my neck while I slept. I saw no alternative other than to sleep with all of my blankets tucked high up over my neck, forever. As an added precaution, I attempted to stay awake as close to dawn as possible. This ensured that any vampire circling our house would fly back to its coffin for the day and leave me un-fanged.

I reasoned that a sheet was insufficient protection against sharp fangs, but piling on another blanket or two would do the job. I am not certain how I survived sleeping in the suffocating heat of our bedroom with blankets tucked in securely at my feet and sides and up over my chin as well. I may have been near passing out most nights but confident in the fact that no green slime had a chance to dissolve me and any vampires lurking around would just give up and fly away when faced with the solid barrier around my neck. I was safe. My superior survival skills were no match for slime or vampires

.

CHAPTER SEVEN

My Great-Aunt Mable lived on the corner of Tecla and Frazho, just two blocks from our house. She was always old and always an invalid, the cause unknown. The invalid status was more an excuse to be waited on, pitied and the means to manipulate her husband and everyone else within shouting distance. Frank was husband number two. I do not know what happened to husband number one. I suspected he simply walked out the door one day and decided not to come back. That is what I would have done.

Mable was short and fat with a head of pure white hair. Her constant companion, other than Frank who was more a servant and never allowed to venture far, was a Pug dog. She held the poor dog on her lap all the time, cooed in its face, and talked in a baby sing-song voice with her nose next to the dog's flat nose. I think she held the dog all the time because it would have fled along with husband number one at the first possible chance.

Mable was Art Schneider's sister. She had the same high pitched laugh that ended up in a sort of stuck-pig squeal. It made my teeth clench every time she wound up.

She never talked, she whined, "Fraaaank, I need another blaaanket. I'm getting a chiiiill."

Frank silently and dutifully ran to get the blanket to cover her fat legs. Legs that, I am convinced, had become increasingly fatter and weaker from lack of use.

Whenever I ventured a visit, I heard, "Oooo Fraaank! Chrisssy is heeere. Come give Auntie Mable a kissss." She was immobilized in a wheel chair so I could skirt around when I wanted to, which was almost always.

We do not get to choose our relatives, which I think is very unfair. Even as a young girl, I could have done a stellar job and would most certainly have passed on Great-Aunt Mable. And Frank.

Mable and Frank had no children. This was one decision that God most definitely got right. That was the good part. The bad part; Mable thought I was just so cute and she was determined to shower me with attention and special favors. Of course I was cute.

My visits to her house were short walks down the road, quick ins and outs to say, "Hi, Aunt Mable. Hi, Uncle Frank." I ignored the dog. I hated that stupid dog. It was not the dog's fault that it had that flat face that Aunt Mable kept kissing, but still, that was just nasty.

Mable made us tea to drink in delicate china cups when I dropped by for a visit. Well, Frank made the tea, but Mable served it with pomp and ceremony. It was festive and elegant. There was nothing like it at my house. If there had been, I would have had to share it with the whole family and the specialness would not have been the same.

Our house had daily noise and confusion and not usually the good kind. If my father was not angry and shouting orders at one or all of us, then he and my mother were arguing. That was never quiet. We just made speedy exits, either outside or upstairs. The stuffy attic was preferable to being in the middle of an argument. Inevitably, my father spent his rage on my mother only to turn to one of us and become inspired to greater heights of screaming and shouting orders. Having an actual reason for his wrath was superfluous. So, when I could escape even to crazy, fat Aunt Mable and her dog, I usually did so.

Then Frank and Mable moved to Roseville. Just like the Roseville Theater, it was not far in miles, but certainly too far to go for a quick visit or even to ride my bike. Shortly after the move, Aunt Mable said how she missed visits from Little Chrissy. I was the favorite grand-niece and could I come for a visit sometime. I was excited at the thought of getting all that time to myself and being the center of attention, even if I had to put up with that flat-nosed dog and Aunt Mable's pig-squeal voice. So a weekend was arranged. I would go over one Friday and stay overnight until Saturday afternoon.

The day arrived. My mother packed my pajamas and clean clothes. Since I only had one pair of shoes that was no problem. I just wore them. Mable was there to greet me and squeal how happy she was to see me.

"EEEE! We are going to have so much fun. Aren't we, Frank?" She managed to whine the words even in joy.

Frank agreed. Aunt Mable showed me that I could have a room all to myself. It had a small desk and chair, just my size. Frank gave me paper, pencils, scissors and scotch tape. This was my dream come true. I wasted no time in setting up my office, even taping my name on the door to make it official. I moved the little desk right in front of the door opening so any business that might come my way could be done speedy quick.

Aunt Mable occasionally rolled down the hallway in her wheelchair to check on me and did the pig squeal thing, "Oh Fraank! See how cute this is? Isn't she sooo cute, Frank?" Frank agreed that I was adorable.

The afternoon wore on, and it was getting time for dinner. Mable sent Frank to the basement to retrieve something necessary for dinner. Her invalid status forbad using stairs. I suspect her legs were just too fat to make the climb either up or down.

"Do you want to go help Uncle Frank, Chrissy?" Mable asked.

Sure. Down we went and Franked opened the door to a small storage closet. He beckoned me in and shut the door. Silently, he turned off the light.

In our house children did not argue. Children did not question. Children did not disobey. Any breach of the rules was met with immediate and harsh penalties. Children kept silent. And there was never anyone to help you. You were alone.

I endured twenty-four hours in that house with Frank and Mable. A new terror grew in my soul. A new sense of horror never before felt covered my heart, buried itself into my spirit and became something that changed forever the person I might have been. My feet touched hell. The burns and scars were forever a reminder that children are expendable, collateral damage wherever evil lurks.

When my mother picked me up, Mable oohed and aahed over how wonderful it had been to have me there and when could I come again. As we walked out the door, I looked back and Frank put his finger to his lips in the "don't tell" gesture and winked at me. I was never alone in their presence again.

Mable, like Marie, was not ignorant of her husband's depravity. And like Marie, she chose to ignore the unspeakable. Frank was and remained until his death a less than human being, his days on earth evil that lurked, not only around him but going forth to suck in unsuspecting life.

CHAPTER EIGHT

Shortly after my seventh birthday and well into warmer weather, I performed my First Holy Communion. I cannot remember from where our Catholic heritage began. We never attended Mass as an entire family. As we each came of age, which was determined by some heavenly and arbitrary method known only to my mother and father, we would be taken to a weekly Mass at our local Parish, Holy Innocents. The name of our little Parish always brought visions of innocent little children being sacrificed for Jesus. To my mind, it was most noble for those imaginary children, just not something in which I wished to become engaged. I kept my distance from all things holy and tried to avoid going to Mass altogether. When I did go because I had no choice, I went with my father.

I caught on quickly that attending the 6:00 a.m. Mass carried the most benefit for me. It was the only one my father attended, so going along meant I got some time alone with him. Being one on one with my father could be enjoyable. If the time together was an outing away from home, he could be warm and caring. He would even occasionally laugh and tease. But adding even one more element to the mix was like adding gasoline to smoldering coals. And my father was always at the smoldering stage.

After Mass we sometimes stopped for milk and a donut at a coffee shop or breakfast bar. The Priest at the early Mass was short and to the point, which also made for a speedy exit and just one half hour out of my day for being holy. If I was lucky, it could be as little as twenty minutes. Either way, I discovered early on that my dad never noticed if I took a short nap during the brief Mass. Other than the kneeling parts, I was pretty much left undisturbed. Since it was said in Latin, which made me feel very holy, it was easy to be lulled off to sleep. The good parts came as you got older.

First Holy Communion was the first fun thing we got to do as good Catholic kids. It meant you wore a frilly white dress. The purchase of my lovely, lacy white dress had been discussed and pondered for quite some time among female relatives, with various aunts giving advice and opinion. And to make it even more glamorous, all the girls wore veils. Mine had a little flower crown with sheer nylon that hung quite beautifully down my back. I spent considerable amounts of time at a mirror, peering over my shoulder to admire how the gossamer material hung down my back.

We had all been instructed by the Nuns on what to wear and what not to wear. Specifically, all the girls were to dress in all white, no exceptions. The boys were to wear dark pants, blue or black, white shirts and little black ties, no exceptions.

My ensemble was progressing satisfactorily until it came time for shoes. I did not own white shoes. My only shoes were ugly and brown. This became a problem. From somewhere or someone a pair of pastel blue shoes just my size appeared. I was told that the blue shoes would be good enough. My mother tried to argue the point with my father. I knew how that would turn out. The days before this major event in my life suddenly became one long nightmarish vision of me walking down the church aisle in BLUE shoes. I was certain that every pair of eyes in the church would look down at my feet and someone would cry out, "Oh no! Stop her! Blue shoes! Sinner!" The magic of the day was not going to be the same. I did not think wearing blue shoes at communion was a mortal sin, but you just never knew.

Every minute of the event had been choreographed by the Nuns in the weeks leading up to this rite of passage. The Nuns left no detail to chance and spent considerable time explaining exactly how to hold our hands in a prayerful way– and where.

"Keep your elbows firmly placed at your sides. Do not bow them out like a turkey flapping its wings." Sister demonstrated a turkey flapping its wings. No one laughed. This was serious business. "And keep your palms together." This command was accompanied by a loud slap for emphasis as Sister demonstrated using her own hands.

"Now, boys and girls keep your fingers straight up, tight together and do not cross your thumbs." This was getting stressful. "With your hands folded in prayer, keep your head bowed low but do not let your nose touch your fingers," she said. "That is too low. Now I want each of you to try it."

We all began practicing not being a turkey with wings, slapping our hands together, fingers straight, thumbs uncrossed and heads bowed, but not too low. I never thought that getting one communion wafer would be so exhausting. I could feel my stomach constrict trying to remember just how to do this and already worried that I would make some horrible mistake.

And then, just when I was getting comfortable with the hands and head rules, Sister got even more serious and talked about the communion wafer itself.

"Father will place the wafer on your tongue. It is smaller than a quarter. You are to swallow the communion wafer. Do not let it touch your teeth and do not ever, ever chew the wafer," Sister paused and gave us her most serious stare. "Remember that you are receiving the actual body of Christ," she continued.

I was getting dizzy, and terrified that my teeth might actually come in contact with God. Panic was setting in and threatened to take over.

"The wafer may stick to the roof of your mouth. Do NOT use your finger to aid in swallowing the wafer. And NEVER touch the wafer." This was all said in a low growl to emphasize her point.

This was too much. I could envision the many ways that I could possibly make mistakes and be barred from Catholicism forever.

Or worse, maybe it was a reason God sent you to Hell. It would occupy my mind for all the days leading up to Communion Sunday.

The day arrived. We all lined up as instructed at the back of the church waiting for the signal. My heart was pounding, just knowing that all the girls with white shoes were staring at my horrible sacrilege of wearing blue shoes. I wanted to hide my feet. I wanted to tell them it was not my fault that my shoes were blue and not white like theirs. I waited for one of the Nuns to grab me by the veil and throw me out into the parking lot. That did not happen.

With my hands folded reverently as instructed, and for which I had practiced daily prior to the event, I lined up with all the other holy, nicely dressed boys and girls. We marched tall and proud, while also appearing humble, to the front of the church and into the first pew. Sitting in the front pew was a first for me. It was much easier to sleep undetected in the back pew. It was also the only place my dad ever sat. But this was a magnificent day, and we were the main event. The big moment finally arrived.   Halfway through the Mass the rows of Communion newbies rose in unison. We left the spot light pew, lined up with hands folded prayerfully at our chest; our heads bowed in reverence, and marched up one by one to the Priest. When I was face to face with the Priest, I raised my head and stuck out my tongue. It took a little work, but I managed to swallow the wafer after using my tongue to get it unstuck from the roof of my mouth. The whole thing went off without a hitch, blue shoes and all.

As nice as that was, the real event was the party after church. For a small child growing up Catholic, this rite of passage was the payoff for sitting through a Mass you could not understand and weeks of Saturday catechism. My parents had cleaned out the garage for the big day. It was swept, the concrete floor hosed down and tables brought in on which would set the feast prepared by my mother. Every relative you knew and some you did not know or could not remember, came to the big day.

Early that morning my father called for me. "Christine, let's go out and pick the spot for the extra chairs and tables in the garage."

This was a strange request. Why was my father asking me for an opinion? No one had ever solicited my opinion on matters before. I certainly had opinions on almost everything, but my ideas and solutions thus far had never been sought. This was a pity as far as I was concerned, because my ideas were always creative and most often the perfect solution.

We walked outside and stood in front of the garage. My father stooped to grab the rusty handle and raise the heavy door up over his head. Slowly his reason for having me there was revealed. A brand new lime-green Schwinn bicycle was setting in the center of the garage. I screamed and my father laughed. There it was, the bicycle of my dreams. No more riding half broken or perpetually in need of repair, hand-me-downs. It was my very own. I have two distinct memories of that bike. The first was seeing it for the first time on that day and the second was an incident that taught me what real fear was all about.

Riding my bike was the greatest thing to do on a warm, breezy day. My streamers flew, and I was certain people were in awe of my bike riding skills. Part of my allowed neighborhood travels was riding the seven or eight blocks down the sidewalks to McGregor's Drugstore. McGregor's sat next to Sy's Market, the neighborhood market. Going to the A&P was reserved for payday and the big load of food. Everything else was purchased at Sy's Market. I had never actually met anyone called Sy, but Nicky insisted he was a real man and had even seen him in person. I trusted that he was telling me the truth. McGregor's was the most fun because we could travel there by ourselves. But then, my friends and I pretty much traveled alone wherever the mood called as long as we did not exceed our boundary limits. McGregor's Drugstore had comic books, which I loved, and chocolate cokes made at the soda fountain. It gave me great pleasure to sit at the soda counter on the twisty red stool sipping a fizzy chocolate coke.

One particular Saturday I managed to scrape together the seven cents for a chocolate coke by rummaging through my father's recliner. His nightly post-dinner naps with the recliner tilted as far back as possible meant bounty the next day. This Saturday I hit pay dirt. Jumping on my bike, with a shout to my mother, off I went. Three or four blocks into my ride, which I was sure was a marvel to behold for anyone observing me, I slowed down to watch a boy sitting on the walkway. He was dirty and unkempt. Not dirty like after a good day of playing outside, but dirty from not washing, changing clothes or bathing. As I stared, pondering what this kid was doing, suddenly out of nowhere, an older, taller and heavier set boy ran at me screaming. As I turned to look, he came, arms flaying with a switch in hand. It was a small, thin sharp stick from a willow tree. I realized he was headed for me. I was his target.

He began to hit me again and again, all the while screaming, "Why are you looking at my friend?"

Every blow stung into my flesh. I stumbled and fell off my bike, getting scraped in the bargain. As suddenly as it began, it ended. He stopped hitting me, stared at me one last time, turned and left. I was hysterical. Sobbing and stumbling, I gathered up my bike and rode back home. My father was in the yard working. Seeing me screaming, peddling and falling, my father ran to the front of our yard to meet me. In between sobs, I managed to relay what had happened. No, I did not know who the boy was. No, I did not do anything to provoke him.

In the midst of this fray, which my neighbors surely looked upon as great drama and something not to be missed, Janet Pechacek came from next door. Having heard my wails through open windows, she rose to the occasion, ready to fight the foe. Janet, two years my senior was tall for her age and built for brute force. Janet brooked no quarter for bullies who picked on weaker children. Although, I suspected she had learned to bully with the best as a necessary skill while living in The Projects. In my mind, and I was certain I was correct in my assumptions, the strange and mysterious world of The Projects was where true evil lived, roaming about looking for innocent victims. So it was logical to me that Janet had honed her skills in order to deal with life in The Projects.

This day Janet presented herself to my dad in full fighting mode. My sobs were the kind that racked my chest, making it difficult to breath and almost impossible to talk. Adding to that, the terror I was experiencing rendered me incoherent.

Barely taking the time to listen, Janet leaned into my father's face, "Joe, you want me to beat him up? I can go find the kid right now, Joe."

She raised her clenched fist to emphasize that the kid had no chance. I believed her.

My father drove down the blocks, taking me along to identify the bully but he was nowhere to be found. The strange boy was gone as well. No marker remained to alert others to the horrific attack.

Even today I am puzzled as to why. Truly I had done nothing to provoke the assault. It was my first, but far from last, introduction to a world of senseless evil over which I would have no control. More than aimless brutality, the palpable fear

Christine and Janet, 1954

that enveloped me or my first taste of panic, what lingers is the sweet memory of Janet rushing to my aid. She threw aside caution and self-preservation for someone weaker. She gave no thought to herself. What a precious thing.

As the years passed and the darkness that would consume us all continued to grow, that part of Janet died. How very sad. I still remember that Janet and am sad for the person once budding inside of her.

CHAPTER NINE

I decided that it would be a good thing to avoid my usual route to McGregor's Drugstore after my experience with the crazy kid and the willow stick. That left me without a place for my favorite chocolate coke. My neighborhood had expanded. I now had friends who lived in some of the new houses and that increased my boundaries. We lived on Frazho Road, also known at 10 ½ Mile Road. Some of my new friends lived on several of the dirt roads running north and south, ending at Ten Mile Road.

Venturing out to succeeding roads also brought me closer to Ten Mile Road and the businesses there. My lime-green Schwinn went up and down the side roads and finally to Ten Mile Road. I was allowed to ride my bicycle to Ten Mile, staying between Firwood and Hayes Road, which gave me a total of four blocks. Johnny's was on Ten Mile Road.

Johnny's Shoe Shop was on Ten Mile Road and since his shop happened to be within my boundary zone, it was a frequent stop on my travels. My brother and I did not own dress shoes, play shoes and school shoes. We each owned one pair of shoes. They were expected to last. Although I do remember an occasional hole in the sole and water or mud coming in on my socks, I did not resort to putting paper inside my shoe to keep my feet dry. Well, only until I could get to Johnny's. I wanted more shoes but so far that had not happened and I could not think of a solution to this problem. It did occur to me one day that if an extra pair of shoes was not going to happen, then maybe I would try for a new pair altogether. Just walking up to my father and asking for a new pair of shoes was out of the question. Some things were so crazy that it did not even bear thinking about. No, I needed to convince my parents, actually my father, whose grip on the family's resources was unyielding, that new shoes were necessary. Sitting on our small concrete porch one afternoon the perfect solution popped right into my head. I would make a tear in my shoes, which would lead my father to say, "Shirley, go buy this child some new shoes!"

It seemed simple enough. Sneaking behind our house where I could not be seen, I picked and dug at the seam on my leather shoe until a small rip appeared. Later I showed my mother the hole, certain we would immediately go shoe shopping. Instead, I got a quarter and was sent on my bicycle to Johnny's Shoe Shop to have the tear I had so cleverly manufactured stitched back together. My shoes were genuine leather, with leather soles and heels, and meant they lasted an eternity and could be repaired over and over again.

Johnny's was an older house turned into a shoe repair shop. Wooden steps lead up to a large wrap-around porch. The front door was heavy and required both my hands to pull it open. The entry way and front room had been converted into the front of the shop. On one wall were shelves with all colors of shoe polish, liquid and wax, cloths for shoe shines and laces of every length but limited colors. Boot laces were long and leathery, but the others were cloth, in brown, black and some white. Off to another side was a wooden counter where you plopped your shoes to be examined under the skillful eyes of Johnny himself. After a minute or two, he declared his judgment call. A price was quoted along with a scheduled pick-up time. Occasionally the job was small enough that you could sit on one of the wooden benches across from the counter and wait for your shoes. This was one of those times.

Johnny took the shoe I had put on the counter and examined the tear. He looked me squarely in the eye for a minute and said, "Twenty-five cents, ten minutes."

I was sure his professional eye could tell that the tear in my shoe had been an inside job. And he must have seen my quarter. I turned and sat down on the empty wooden bench, my quarter securely in hand. The bench was a tall one, or so it seemed to me. My feet did not touch the floor when I sat back so I let them swing back and forth. While I waited, I stared at the racks and racks of shoes behind the counter, all out of reach but not out of sight. Each had a tag attached. No names, just numbers on each tag. The customer got one half and Johnny attached the other half to the shoe. You only got your shoes if the numbers matched. I did not know what happened if you lost your half of the ticket. But I was certain Johnny would under no circumstances give out a shoe without the required matching ticket, which led me to wonder what he did with one lone shoe.

Sure enough, ten minutes later I heard the PLOP of my shoes on the counter. Johnny had taken both shoes for two reasons. He checked both shoes to make sure no other repairs were needed, and your shoes always got a free shine before you got them back. Well shine or no shine, they were the same shoes I had come in with, brown leather. Brown, ugly leather. The only difference was the new clean stitching along the side of one, and they were now polished and shiny. Big deal. I was still not happy about my shoes. I put my quarter on the counter and mumbled a thank you. Johnny just stared at me. I was sure that he knew I had sabotaged my own shoes. I stared right back. I went out the door, down the wooden steps, hopped on my lime-green Schwinn and hoped my shoes got good and dirty on the way home.

Brown's Dairy was another one of my newly acquired destinations. It was the local dairy and ice cream parlor. A very modern drive-up window had been added so it was no longer necessary to go inside to buy milk. My mother bought milk in one gallon glass bottles, three at a time. Each bottle had a small round paper topper. Bringing back clean empty bottles meant you got credit for the next bottle deposits on your milk purchase. We would drive up to the outside window, put the wire basket of clean empty bottles on the ledge and wait while the girl in the window replaced them with three full bottles and then took our money. That was okay, but what I really enjoyed was riding up on my Schwinn to go inside for a hot fudge Sundae at the counter. It was all very grown up and made me feel sophisticated. Brown's Dairy did not sell chocolate cokes however, so when a new drugstore came to town I was excited.

McGregor's had been the one and only drug store as far back as I could remember, and we did not ever imagine such an overthrow could occur. But this recent drugstore, Cassidy's, was new and curiosity got the best of me. Cassidy's Drugs became one of my travel stops along Ten Mile Road. It had the same soda fountain with one exception. McGregor's stools sat high on an elevated stand and it required that you step up onto the stand and then hop up on a stool. Cassidy's had come along and put the stools flat on the floor. It was very avant-garde for the neighborhood. You just walked up to the stool and sat right flat on the thing. This was going to take some getting used to. I soon became a frequent visitor to Cassidy's. Every time I got money for a chocolate coke, I made my way to the flat-on-the-floor soda fountain stools at Cassidy's. And just like McGregor's the stools twirled around. That was good.

One Saturday I was wandering the store looking at perfume (which I had never owned) and jewelry (which was too grown up for me and I could not buy anyway), when I came across a girl counting jelly beans and putting them into a huge glass jar. I thought it very strange indeed, so I stopped to watch. I listened to her as she counted out loud each jelly bean. It was boring so I went on my way, drank my chocolate coke on the flat-on-the-floor stool and rode my lime-green Schwinn bicycle home.

The next Saturday I was again at Cassidy's, this time with my girlfriend, Linda. In the middle of a very persuasive argument as to why she should buy me a box of cough drops, I stopped dead in my tracks. There it was. A giant glass jar full of jelly beans. The sign next to it said, "GUESS THE NUMBER OF JELLY BEANS

AND WIN A KODAK FLASH CAMERA." Well now, wasn't this a twist of fate? My curiosity just might pay off with a new camera. I stood and thought back to the girl counting jelly beans a few days ago. My ability to remember useless information was going to come in handy. The small white slip of paper next to the jar asked for my name, phone number and my guess of the number of jelly beans. I was ready. Very carefully and neatly I printed: CHRISTINE WENER, Prescott 6-4338 and my guess for the jelly beans that I remembered with a few added. Then I went back to pester Linda for a fountain coke.

A few days later my mother asked me if I had entered a jelly bean contest.

"Yes," I said.

"Well, apparently you won some prize," she said.

Wow. It was the first contest I had ever won. It was also to be the last. Perhaps the fact that I never, ever, won anything else was punishment for taking undue advantage and using my super-remembering brain in the jelly bean contest. But for then, I was happy. I had a brand new, blue, Kodak flash camera. It took me a few days to pester my mother enough until she gave in and gave me money for film and flashbulbs. The film came on two small cylinders, one with film, the other empty. After each picture, you turned the black knob and it rolled to the next stop for a new picture. Numbers appeared in a tiny window on the back of the camera so you knew when to stop the roll. Otherwise, you would roll right by and waste a picture. When all the film had been shot, the little knob would not turn. This new and very modern, Kodak had the flash attachment built right into the camera. The bulbs were bigger than I had seen before. Each one looked like a small light bulb but instead of screwing them in, you just pushed until it popped in place. Film came in twelve or twenty-four shots. The flash bulbs were not included so that purchase took extra negotiation on my part. I believe my mother referred to this as whining.

Armed with my new camera, film, and flash bulbs I set out to become a stalking picture taking champion. Aiming at unsuspecting persons, I would shout, "Hey! Smile!" and 'POP' the flash went off. The bulbs caused momentary blindness for the subject from the intense, bright light. It made a sizzling sound, leaving the spent bulb bubbled from the sudden heat of its flash. Removing the hot bulb was risky.

"Christine, wait until the bulb cools down before you take it out. You are going to burn your fingers," my mother advised me, as I hopped around in pain blowing on my fingertips.

Eventually I did leave my picture taking phase but only because I ran out of money for film.

CHAPTER TEN

During summer months, Alwood Elementary School had a recreation program for all the neighborhood kids. There were craft days when, for a dime, you could make a braided bracelet out of leather strips of different colors. That was my favorite activity of all. There were other crafts besides my beloved leather work, such as papier-mâché decorations, but that was messy. The glue ended up all over my clothes and the paper stuck to my hands, giving me blue, red and green fingers from the dye. I was never successful at papier-mâché.

I did try the Popsicle stick genre. But there never seemed to be anything new and original to do with Popsicle sticks. No matter what I did with them, it ended up being just a flat something or other. They could line up and be a lot of flat sticks stuck together or just one flat stick with buttons glued on for eyes. It was obvious that Popsicle crafting was not my artistic gift. Even though I found the Popsicle stick art form boring, I was more than willing to provide all the Popsicle sticks needed for the entire summer craft season by eating as many Popsicles as necessary. I was certain I could do that much.

The ice cream man came down Firwood Road seven days a week in the summer. It was the Good Humor Ice Cream truck to be precise, but we all just called him the ice cream man. He came the same time every day, slowly making his way down the dirt road, the familiar tune playing. No matter where we were or in what fantastic game we were engaged, time stopped the minute we heard the music. Scattering like bees when the nest is kicked, we all ran home for money. My keen hearing picked up the ice cream tune at least two streets away, so I had time to run home and search.

My brother and I never had loose change. Every penny was accounted for in our house, in part because there was so little money and also because my father kept track of every expenditure. Bills or change were either in my mother's purse, a forbidden place to put your hands, or in my father's pockets. When there was money in my father's pocket, it was the same as having a personal piggy bank. Each night after dinner, my father would sit in his lumpy, gray recliner and sleep for about an hour. Even though he never moved in the recliner, just lying back, mouth open and snoring, all his pocket change slipped out somehow and went down the sides of the recliner. I never understood how, nor did I ever question the process.

When the alert went out that the ice cream man was on the way, it was my job to run home. Storming through the front door, I dropped to my knees at my father's recliner and start digging for change. I only ever withdrew from the chair bank what we needed for that day. Nicky and I always wisely left some for the next day of ice cream. By this time, I only had minutes to run out the door, across our front lawn, through Pechacek's back yard, and through the ditch to where, by now, a small mob of kids stood waiting for the Good Humor ice cream truck to round the corner.

On the rare occasion when we were caught unawares and the ice cream truck was inching down the road away from our spot, we all ran after him furiously screaming, "Ice cream man! Ice cream man! STOP! STOP!" Thank goodness for rear view mirrors and his keen sense of hearing. He always stopped, but as far as we were concerned, it was touch and go.

I got the same thing every time, the lime and raspberry Popsicle, my favorite. The raspberry side had little bits of red raspberry in it. But the lime side was my *very* favorite. I tried to save it until last but it was hard to eat one side of a Popsicle at a time. Once in a while I broke with tradition and got an orange Creamsicle. That was good but not as good as the lime-raspberry Popsicle. These frozen works of art, my love of them, and my father's recliner chair bank were the reasons I could supply the summer recreation program with all the Popsicle sticks ever needed should someone ask.

In addition to my love for the magnificent lime-raspberry Popsicle, my favorite thing to do at summer recreation was to go to Metropolitan Beach for the whole day. As many kids as a school bus could hold would ride to the beach located on Lake St. Clair at 16 Mile Road and Jefferson. Nicky and I would plan it all out: we would get permission slips from my mother, pack a lunch, usually consisting of peanut butter and jelly sandwiches, get our bathing suits and towels ready and obtain two quarters. This money came from my mother's purse so there was no need to go to the gray lumpy recliner bank for money. The quarter covered something to drink at lunch and a deposit on a small locker at the beach pavilion. Everyone got a locker key that was attached to a wrist band. The locker was where we put our clothes and shoes while we were at the beach. On the bus ride to the beach I usually sat with my friend LaVerne. But sometimes, my best friend, Pam, went too and then I would sit with her. The friend hierarchy was not something with which you messed.

Metropolitan Beach was a wonderful place with sand as far as you could see and the water stayed shallow for what seemed to me, a long way out. We would go in up to our waist and jump, scream, and splash water at each other. I did not know how to swim so venturing out very far was not something I considered. And although I was certain the Creature from the Black Lagoon was not at Metropolitan Beach, there seemed no good reason to take undue risk. I stayed close to shore.

When it was lunch time, one of our adult chaperones blew a whistle and a mob of kids ran to shore. We grabbed our towels, ran across sand hot enough to cook an egg and ate our bagged lunch under umbrellas on the beach patio area. After lunch, we were all instructed to wait one hour before going back into the water. Having been warned that any less of a wait time would result in cramping so horrific you would be swept under and out into the nether regions of Metropolitan Beach, I stayed as far back as possible from the water for the full sixty minutes. For all I knew, the Black Lagoon Creature was out there waiting for some unsuspecting kid he could grab and take to his underwater cave. At the end of the day, we piled back into the bus, sunburned, full of sand, and exhausted for the ride home.

Almost all the kids in the neighborhood went on beach day. Other than playing in the ditches in front of our houses after a hard rain, there was no water around the neighborhood. But ditch playing was more of a winter sport in our neighborhood anyway.

Frazho Road had deep ditches in front of the houses and to us they were there for playing. A dry ditch was perfect for riding my bike in and out, over and over, faster and faster. And when it rained heavily and the ditch filled up, it was for hunting frogs, watching things float by and walking down the middle in boots, hoping you did not sink too low and get soakers. I had rubber boots that pulled straight over my shoes and came mid-way up my shin. I had to tug hard and stomp my foot until the boot finally went over my shoe. Getting them off was no easier. My shoes always came off with the boot and I had to tug and pull my shoe out. It was a lot of work but still, I loved walking in the ditches. Winter was the best time for ditch-walking. The water froze and I could slip and slide down the ditch until a driveway, hop out, cross the driveway, hop back down and move on. It was fun until the ice broke and my feet went into the icy-cold water.

One particular morning I was making my way to school, slipping and sliding in the ditch when the ice broke. This ditch was particularly deep. The water went up to my knees and filled over into my boots. Deciding I had no choice, it was cold and I was wet, I headed home to change. I knew I would be in serious trouble because of something I had often heard.

My mother warned us every winter day when we left for school, "Stay out of the ditches. You'll get wet," she would say.

"Ok, we will," Nicky hollered back as we both ran out the door, across the yard, through Pechacek's back yard and onto the ice covered ditch.

Even though my mother became irritated each time we fell through into the icy water, she helped us change. Then, dressed and dry once again, we went back to walking on the ice covered ditches.

On this particular day, I trudged back home, crying from the cold and not wanting to hear my mother be angry at me for falling into the forbidden ditch. My father was home. The construction site he was working on must have shut down for the day for some reason or other. His work was weather dependent so it was not unusual for him to be home at odd hours during the day. I felt my stomach lurch and started crying harder. I was terrified and I knew this was not going to be a good day.

When I finally got back home, my father took me into the tiny bathroom, sat me down on the toilet lid and started stripping off my icy, wet clothes. He stopped, sniffed, and turned to my mother.

"Jesus Christ, Shirley!" he shouted. "This kid smells like piss. Did you let her go to school smelling like this?"

"Well I didn't smell anything when she got up," my mother said.

"How the hell could you not smell it? She reeks," my father continued to shout. "Did you wet the bed?" he asked me.

"Yes," I said in my quiet voice. I had been wetting my bed nightly for so long I could not remember waking up in a dry bed.

"Did you check her sheets?" He asked my mother.

"No, not this morning," her voice was sliding close to defiant.

I felt familiar the panic that surfaced whenever their voices rose. As with each fight between them, I wanted to run and hide from the conflict. I wanted to be someplace safe and away from the chaos.

"You have to check every morning, Shirley," he said. "Why in the hell would you not check?" He was standing now, looking at my mother.

"Yes, I know I should. I will, Joe. I'll make sure next time," she spoke softly. The important thing was to shut him up and defuse the storm. My mother knew that.

Bedding was washed once a week with all the other laundry, on Monday. In between, I just pulled back the covers and let my bed air out for the day. On the rare occasions when I woke up in the middle of the night and felt the pool of urine under me, I got up and grabbed a towel to put over the wet sheet. But mostly, I slept right through and had no memory of wetting my bed. And, other than occasionally such as this morning, no one seemed to notice or care.

The shouting and blaming that ensued, which was normal for almost any day, was one-sided. My father did the shouting and blaming and my mother remained tearfully silent. And as usual, it ended with my mother in tears, my father muttering under his breath, and then silence. I was scrubbed down, got my clothes changed and off to school I went, thankful to be out of the house and out of the range of my father's rage for the day.

I went back to walking in the ditches all down Firwood Road to school. This time, I stepped more carefully.

CHAPTER ELEVEN

My love for chocolate was no secret. Easter was my favorite holiday, not because Jesus rose from the grave, which I rarely gave thought to, but because we all got great baskets of chocolate candy. I enjoyed Halloween but not every house you went to handed out chocolate. And each Halloween after I had done the work of going street after street and dragging home the pillowcase weighed down with candy, plus whatever else the adults threw in my bag, my father insisted on checking my take for bad stuff as he called it. This was his way of finding choice pieces of candy and then eating them. He did not fool me. My father was a chocolate lover as well. It did no good to argue. Taking a stand of any kind for any reason against my father was never a wise thing to do. What sometimes began as kidding or playful wrestling on the floor more often than not ended up with my father erupting into a fit of rage. He could go from happy to rage in the time it took to flip a switch. My siblings and I never knew why or what triggered the explosion, but since we were there at the time, it seemed logical that we were the cause. As a result we spent most of our childhood trying to be invisible and silent.

I am not sure why my Easter take was never pilfered, but it was left alone by everyone except my brother, Nicky. He and I both, upon finding our hidden baskets and then carefully memorizing the contents, took them away to store under our beds. As the days wore on and all the best candy was consumed, Nicky would make his way to my basket to ferret out any morsels now buried and stuck to the Easter grass. Candy was not a necessity to my parents. Although we thought they were gravely mistaken in this regard, it was unlikely we would find any tucked away in our cupboards. We knew because we had looked. However, sweets in the form of baked goods were an entirely different story.

My mother enjoyed cooking and in particular, baking. I remember delicious smells coming from the kitchen when I was very young. Pies were some of her most magnificent creations. One dish in particular was her best production, and it was not a cake or pie. It was beef stew.

The stew was first cooked on top of the stove in a large cast iron pot. Bits and pieces of stew meat got dropped into sizzling hot oil to brown and seal in the juices. The crackle and pop of the grease always meant something good on the way. Unlike my father, who stood near sizzling oil, daring it to strike him, my mother was more cautious. Besides wearing an apron, she was careful to stand back as she dropped the pieces of meat into the hot oil.

After the stew had cooked most of the day, simmering slowly and occasionally stirred, it was ready for the final touch and my favorite part. The table was cleared for biscuit making. Out came flour, Crisco, salt, milk and baking powder. I liked to watch as the ingredients became sticky dough in my mother's big yellow mixing bowl. Next, reaching into the bin to grab a handful of flour, my mother skillfully tossed it onto the table to make a kind of flour desert in the middle of the Formica table. The blob of dough got dropped onto the flour desert for rolling. A huge, wooden rolling pin was kept in a drawer with other baking utensils and brought forth with what I saw as great ceremony. The rolling pin fascinated me because it was never washed in hot soapy water like the other baking utensils. When I asked why, my mother told me the water would strip the roller of all the good oils that had seeped in over the years of rolling out the different dough. Each time she finished with the rolling pin, she carefully wiped it with a damp cloth to remove any flour or Crisco and put it back in its coveted position.

Back and forth went the roller over the dough with occasional sprinkles of flour until it was evenly flattened to one half to three-quarters of an inch. Next, the biscuit cutter was produced; a round flute-edged metal cup with a red wooden handle on top for lifting after the cut had been made into the dough. Cut after cut proceeded until a dozen or more biscuits lay on the flour desert. Finally, the biscuits were placed on top of the now thickened stew simmering on the stovetop. This all went into the oven until the biscuits were high, fluffy and golden brown. When it was dinnertime, each scoop of stew put on a plate was topped by a delicious biscuit. I often dreamed that someday, when I had my own home and family, I would create this masterpiece and wanted my mother to teach me just how to do it.

But that never happened. My mother's life, and consequently ours as well, was slowly fading away into some dark and dangerous abyss from which there would be no recovery. Perhaps it was just as well that, as children, evil was still largely foreign to our world and to our way of thinking.

Our kitchen, my mother's hub of activity, was always clean. The floor with the dark brown tile squares had dots of yellow and gold and seemed to us to be perpetually shiny. But it was my mother's hard work that made it so. She began with a metal bucket of hot, soapy water and two towels, one to wash and one to soak up the dirty water. Next, came a bucket of clean warm water to wipe up any remaining soap. The floor was allowed to dry before the next and final step, applying a coat of wax. As she did with the washing, this was done on hands and knees making certain every corner and crevice was clean. Finally, a clean damp cloth was used to spread liquid wax in small circular motions. The wax dried to a high a polished sheen, reflecting your face back to you. At least I was sure I could see my own face.

Our refrigerator, a huge white box, took up a sizeable portion of wall space in the kitchen. The freezer space was a part of the entire refrigerator, only separated by its own door. The freezer required defrosting occasionally when the ice built up to form deep crusts on the sides. Defrosting the freezer was an arduous and all day task. This particular condition was caused, and made worse, by repeatedly opening and closing the refrigerator door, or standing with the door open staring aimlessly into the refrigerator. I think I held the record for the most openings and closings for no good reason. Whether I was bored, actually hungry, or sometimes just passing through the kitchen, I stopped, opened the refrigerator door and paused while I contemplated its contents.

"What are you looking for?" my mother said, having an innate ability to hover and so view my every move, unbeknownst to me.

"Just looking." My surprised reply came without thinking. It was just one of my stock answers.

"Well, don't stand with the door open." My response to this was always to shrug; sigh deeply and dramatically, and slowly shut the large, heavy door.

However, my frequent stops to peer into the refrigerator sometimes paid off when I would actually see a morsel of interesting left-over or a piece of fruit, which I would quickly eat. But my greatest find came the day I discovered carefully hidden pieces of chocolate. My mother obviously thought this ruse would keep me away from the prize chocolate.

At the back of the refrigerator, second shelf, tucked behind some non-descript items, there it was. It was a wrapper I had never seen before, blue and white with orange writing. The small box slid open to reveal chocolate wrapped in tiny, tinfoil squares. I looked over my shoulder to make certain no one lurked unseen and that my mother was not hovering out of sight. The coast was clear. Carefully and quietly opening the tinfoil, I broke off three or four squares and popped them into my mouth. There was no time to slowly savor the taste. I clenched down on cold, hard squares of chocolate. The bitter taste surprised me, but chocolate was chocolate and I was not going to miss out. Satisfied that I had gotten away with my latest discovery, I wrapped the remaining squares and put the evidence back in place so my mother would never know. I was clever and especially pleased at my find since my brother, Nicky, was not here to grab some. Eyeing the box one last time so I could remember where it was hidden, I made special note of the unfamiliar name on the box: EX-LAX.

I never ate cold chocolate again.

CHAPTER TWELVE

My siblings and I lived under the same roof but existed in our own personal and separate vacuum worlds. We had no head to look to for stability or leadership and no shadow of protection under which to hide or find solace. We found no shelter where we could hide from the storms of anger. Our parents provided no foundation of stability or security. Our family resembled a circus side show game of chance. Like the little plastic ducks passing by in a shooting gallery, my siblings and I never knew when the next hit would ring out. From youngest to oldest, every day was a crap shoot of fear, insanity, and helplessness.

My younger sister, Shirley Ann, was tiny with huge dark eyes and short dark brown hair that barely covered her ears, making her crop of hair resemble a nice little bowl. We did not share much other than the heat of our stifling attic bedroom. Shirley was named after my mother.

To have the same name as a parent always seemed unfortunate to me. One of my best friends was named after her mother and her brother, after his dad. We called them Big LaVerne and Little LaVerne, Big Tony and Little Tony. I thought that was a silly way to go through life and was glad I had a name all to myself. Occasionally we heard Big Shirley or Little Shirley when someone wanted to refer to my sister or mother but then we just permanently called my sister Shirley Ann. Baby Michael came along when she was six years old and threw her into middle child status. Shirley Ann was quiet and compliant. In our house, those two attributes contributed to survival. In fact, being silent and invisible as a kid in the Wener household became necessities of life. Shirley Ann was soft and sweet with a tender heart, and never more so than when it came to family pets.

Our backyard was long and narrow, part yard and part field. Our dog Neil was a black and white springer of questionable parentage. Poor Neil had to live in a fenced-in area for his whole life. He was not allowed in the house, and we never took him out of his pen to play. Attached to Neil's fenced-in area was a wooden shed. In the shed were bales of straw that were used to line the rabbit cages. My father had built two rabbit pens and we had several rabbits at any given time inside the pens. The two cages stood side by side, about three feet off the ground with one roof covering both cages. The rabbits were ignored for the most part, just like poor Neil. One of us would be forced to feed and water the rabbits each day. My sister had a particular fondness for our rabbits and spent time talking to them and petting them.

Then tragedy struck. Some small animal managed to get inside the cage and kill one of the rabbits. Most unfortunately, it was one to which my sister had a definite attachment. It hit her hard. My father and sister went under the roof of the cage while she sobbed, and my father, down on one knee, attempted to explain to her the harsh realities of being lower on the food chain in life. I am not certain she ever fully understood the concept. Shirley Ann was the sibling who quietly took care of helpless creatures.

My mother watched and monitored what came around Shirley Ann, and what she brought into the house. We had a dark colored coffee table that set in front of our gray couch. On top of the coffee table were a few pieces of bric-a-brac which set on top of crocheted doilies. Each of the white doilies had been made by Grandma Marie. She made them in various sizes and each one with a different and intricate design. All were starched and carefully ironed. Some had wavy patterns and some high puffy sides that, with enough starch, stood high and solid, inflexible as an iceberg floating in the ocean. Directly in the middle of one puff of white threads set my parents' china cigarette holder.

This was the middle 50s and, as was the norm, everyone smoked. People bought cigarettes in packs, opened the packs and put the loose cigarettes into a china or wooden container set out for guests. It was very modern. My parents did not have guests who came over and smoked the cigarettes left in the china container, but it was there anyway. This particular container was two shades of green; dark green on the bottom and a lighter shade of green on the lid. The lid also had two pink sculpted roses with green leaves which were used as the handle. I liked the way it looked. It made our ordinary living room look as though we often had guests, which we did not.

On one particular warm sunny day, the living room seemed to have an odor that could not be identified. My mother did her sniff search, walking around the room, sniffing in corners, furniture, and curtains to try and locate the source of the odor. Stopping at the coffee table, she sniffed harder several times and slowly leaned over until she was inches away from the lovely green dish on top of the fluffy doily. My mother lifted the lid and found earth worms in varying degrees of decay. Shirley Ann thought they had been in need of shelter, warmth and rescue. Since they were all beyond help by this time, my mother tossed away the dead worms.

My father once told Shirley Ann that she had been found under a piece of cabbage in the garden, and he just decided to keep her. We had a garden of sorts at the time so she believed him. She cried and kept saying it could not be true but with the garden right there, the evidence seemed pretty compelling.

Shirley Ann was quiet and shy and for me, that meant an easy target. As a young girl she had what were probably allergies. Sleeping in a hot, dusty, airless attic with sheets of insulation exposed over our heads was probably not the ideal environment for her. Often at night she would cough and be unable to stop. The spasms increased and lasted longer.

One night after what seemed like hours of cough-cough-cough, I told Shirley Ann to stop. It was a simple command.

Cough—cough—cough.

"Stop it!" I said with more force accompanied by a hard shove to her shoulder.

Cough—cough—cough.

This time I turned over and hammered on her. She cried but kept coughing.

Shortly after that incident we were in bed for the night and I felt our shared bed shake and heard a muffled cough-cough-cough. Silence. I had just drifted off to sleep when a sneeze of epic proportions shook the bed and rattled me awake. I turned in time to see bits of bloody Kleenex fly outward from my sister's nose in a long spray. It was gross and so I hit her for that.

Shirley Ann thought if she could keep her nose from running, she would stop sniffling and also stop coughing, thereby avoiding another pounding by me. So it made perfect sense to her to break off tiny pieces of Kleenex and stuff the pieces up her nose until both nostrils were packed tight. It did not stop the sneeze or cough and did not keep her from getting hit by me.

Like the rabbits on the lower rung of the food chain, Shirley Ann was below me. And I, most unfortunately, was below Nicky. Perhaps he thought it necessary to make up for my treatment of Shirley Ann by meting out the same to me. Nicky made a career out of teasing me and terrifying me every chance he got.

My parents occasionally went out for the evening and when they did, Nicky, as the oldest, was in charge. On one such occasion, he kept at me, poking and prodding me until I snapped. I grabbed a large kitchen knife and ran for him. Screaming, he ran for the front door. I followed in hot pursuit, knife high over my head, screaming threats as I went. He flew out the front door. I slammed it behind him and locked it.

After his initial fear wore off, he got angry. "Unlock this door right now!" He screamed. I grinned through the glass.

"I'm not telling you again. Open this damn door!" In our parents absence profanity was often used. I grinned wider and stayed silent. I was enjoying the power I had even though I knew it was temporary.

"I'll break this glass if you don't let me in," his voice low and threatening. I was feeling smug and powerful. I just shook my head slowly and smiled.

He banged on the glass to let me know he meant business. I laughed.

"You better not break the glass," I said.

Not one to take orders from a sister, he thumped the glass one more time, with attitude.

CRASH! The pane of glass shattered and fell through to the floor. I jumped back, looked at the glass on the floor and then at Nicky.

"Oh no. You are in big trouble now," I said in a hushed voice. His eyes were wide open as he realized what he had done.

My brother and I knew how to fight. We could even draw blood at times and certainly leave bruises on one another, but we were first and foremost siblings in a house ruled by anger and punishment. I knew what my father would do to Nicky if he came home and found the broken glass. Nicky knew it too. Every other thought was gone now but how to clean up the mess and agree on a story that sounded plausible. We cleaned up the glass and spent the rest of the time until my parents got home figuring out just how this awful accident happened. Tormentor he may have been, he was still my brother. My stomach knotted and turned imagining what my father would do to Nicky should he find out that what was done had been done in anger. Of course, we had seen my father do similar and worse things in an angry rage many times in our short lives. In the small utility room of our house, there was a doorknob-sized hole in the drywall behind the bathroom door. This was the result of a burst of anger from my father. He had slammed the door against the wall and put the knob through the wall. It remained like that all the time we were in the house.

As a finish carpenter, my father did projects out of our garage. He owned table saws, hammers, nails, and a myriad number of other tools that I could not name. Lumber was everywhere and sawdust carpeted the concrete floor. Occasionally he would need a hand, as he referred to it, and one of us would be conscripted into service. Knees shaking, head low in dread, the unfortunate victim would go out to the garage. This was when Shirley Ann was the favored child. She was too young to help. Entering the dreaded garage was more like entering a new level of *Dante's Inferno.* It was impossible to do anything right. A correct move by the helper did not exist in my father's universe.

Being younger and smaller, I would occasionally be called upon to hold the light as my father put in a screw or measured some obscure spot on a piece of wood. There are not many options as to how to hold a light on one spot but, it seemed, I was adept at doing it wrong every time.

"Stop shining the damn light in my eyes. I can't see a thing." my father said. I quickly shifted the beam again.

"Damn it, Christine!" This time he grabbed the light from my hand, turned it and my hand, and said, "Point it here." He put the light back into my hand, which was now shaking. The familiar anxiety settled in my chest and tears burned my eyes.

"Oh hell. Never mind. Just go." I put the light down and ran out of the garage.

Nicky was called upon when a larger project required assistance. I tried to stay as far away as possible. Before long, inevitably shouts, curses, and the sound of tools and or wood flying through the air and hitting something solid could be heard from the garage. Unfortunately, Nicky did not get expelled from the dreaded garage until either the task was complete or my father went into a full-fledged rage. My mother just never went out there.

Sometimes my father enlisted someone outside the family to help in his garage. From time to time, in the evenings when my mother worked, Milly went to help. His tone during those times was soft, gentle, instructive, quietly correcting mistakes. Milly must have known just exactly where to shine the light because there was never any shouting. Danny, Milly's eldest and just fifteen years old, became a helper as well. Evidently he was also highly skilled because my father was full of praise and thanks for his help.

But regardless of my father's mindless outbursts, he was able to excuse his own anger, making it the only justifiable rage allowed in our home. Staring at the broken glass that afternoon, Nicky and I came up with a story of stumbling, falling against the window causing it to shatter. Inexplicably, it worked. We lived to fight another day. And Nicky owed me big time.

I often escaped my father's wrath regardless of my stupidity. There had been occasions of harsh discipline with the razor strap but for the most part I escaped unscathed. The wooden shed behind our garage that housed straw for the rabbits was a favorite place of mine. It was small and had no windows. I liked to go there sometimes just to sit alone and pretend all sorts of games. On one occasion I was in the shed and found a pack of matches that must have fallen out of my father's shirt pocket. I thought I would just light one to see how it looked in the dark shed. After a couple of tries, one lit, burned my finger and I dropped in into the straw. The dry straw. I stared as a small cloud of smoke came up. The small cloud turned into a flame. I ran screaming from the shed. My father heard my screams, saw the flames and ran for the garden hose.

By the time the fire was under control, most of the contents of the shed were burned up or charred beyond saving. It had not taken long to put the fire out, but the damage was done. I waited for what I thought would be the inevitable punishment. I just wondered how long it would last and how much it would hurt.

My father came over to me and said, "What happened?"

Sobbing, I said, "I don't know." It was always a safe place to start and then depending on my father's reaction and the evidence, I went in slow increments toward the truth.

"Were you playing with matches?" he asked. My father did not shout. It was a quiet question.

I nodded my head and kept crying. For reasons I still do not understand, he closed his eyes and just shook his head. No anger. No shouting.

"Well, it's done. There was a table and chair set in there that belonged to one of your aunts and it was for you. Now it's gone." He stood up and walked away.

A table and chair set would have been nice.

CHAPTER THIRTEEN

Linda was my rich friend. I knew she must be rich because she lived in one of the newly built brick ranch houses on Rosenbush, and her dad parked the family car inside the garage. Our garage was perpetually full of carpentry items. I am certain there had never been a car parked in our garage. Most of the people on Frazho Road did not own a garage and if they did, used them in the same way we did, to store junk. The Stahls, who lived across the street from us, had a large house with an even bigger garage. They used their garage as a factory of sorts. They cut out and sold felt letters. It seemed a silly thing to do as far as I was concerned. Who bought felt letters?

Linda had her own bedroom. It was a real bedroom with a closet for her clothes, of which she had many. There were shelves on one wall that held books and games. I had never seen so many board games in one place outside of a store.

The Weners did not own real board games. Any games we owned were of our own making. However, we did own several decks of playing cards. Adults in our house and most of those who visited our house played Euchre. I learned to play Euchre by standing at the table silently watching and listening. There was a constant cloud of cigarette smoke that hovered in the air over the table.

I think that was when I must have taken up smoking, although I had never held a cigarette in my hand. Still, standing silently to watch adults play Euchre was a nice pastime and taught me a new skill. I felt grown up and just a bit superior because I knew how to play an adult card game. I was not allowed to play Euchre with the adults, but still, if I were ever asked, I could jump right in and play.

Linda and Christine, 1961

It always felt like a step-up in status going to Linda's. I never stood on Linda's porch and screamed her name until she came to the door as I did with my other friends. When visiting most friends' front porch to see if they were home, it was common practice to holler as loud as you could until someone came to the door. The call for a friend consisted of yelling the friend's name repeatedly, without stopping in a sing-song cadence. Some names were suited to the call and my favorite name to scream was my friend LaVerne. I would stand on her porch and yell, LA—VERNE! LA—VERNE!, relentlessly, with the emphasis on the "La" until she appeared. Other names were just not designed to be called in such a great way. If you did not have a two syllable name, it was created for you. For instance, my name was a little difficult, but doable. CAA—RISS! CAA—RISS!! Another good example was Pam, which became PAA—IM! PAA—IM! Linda's name would have been perfect for my system: LIN—DA! LIN—DA! But I never called out Linda's name on her porch because her family actually had a doorbell. It was the big time on Rosenbush.

Linda's house was not only new and modern; it was neat - all the time neat. Linda was an only child, which I thought must be lonely but probably not a lot of work for her mother. The house had three bedrooms, one occupied by her parents, one by Linda, and one that had been turned into a den. That was a room I had only seen on TV and in magazines. Walking down the hall to Linda's bedroom, my eyes were always drawn to the dark, neat, manicured room, mysteriously waiting for a tall businessman to come in and do something important.

Rosenbush was just three blocks down from Frazho Road, making the physical distance between our houses small and insignificant. As were most of my friends, I was allowed to roam our small neighborhood. It never occurred to any of us during those wonderful summer days of childhood how free we were to run and play. My child's mind could not have imagined that the freedom I took for granted then would be left far behind, and replaced by fear and suspicion as I grew.

But physical distance is only one aspect of a friendship. Ours had a deeper distance, one that I doubt either of us could have named. It was the subtle leap from lower to middle class. I do not mean that Linda ever treated me differently, expected less of me as a friend or even hinted at the chasm between our lives. But I knew it because I felt it. It was the unnamed, sometimes palpable line that separated us, not only in material things, but in our culture and the way we lived our lives. I could not define it as a feeling of envy for her clothes, games or even her very new house. Linda lived her life in a different world than I did. As young as we were even then, there was no sameness about our existence. The awareness just floated around me that this family was not like my family; or, for that matter, not like most of the families I knew.

Linda's mother was kind and always appeared pleased to see her only daughter's friends. Occasionally I was invited over to Linda's house for lunch. Our elementary school, Alwood, was newly built and centered in our small neighborhood. No big yellow buses drove the nearby roads and stopped to pick up children. We all marched each morning down new sidewalks to the small, one-story brick building. And because there was no cafeteria, we all walked back home to eat lunch while we watched Soupy Sales on the tiny screen of a black and white television. Afterwards we made a speedy trip back to finish the day at school. The routine was sometimes interrupted by sporadic invitations from friends to eat lunch at their house, which I looked forward to every chance I got.

At Linda's house we sat in the kitchen at a snack bar and not a kitchen table, which was the only option at my house. Their kitchen was small and so there was a real dining room area with a table just for eating. This was a new thing to my way of thinking as well. Our table was used for a variety of activities unrelated to the actual eating of meals, like playing Euchre, for instance. It seemed a waste of open space only to eat at a table, but this was after all, Rosenbush. Sitting at the snack bar eating soup and sandwiches made me feel very formal and required my best table manners. And in that area, I could be counted on to deliver.

At my house around our table, we knew table manners. No talking with your mouth full. Elbows on the table met with a friendly fork jab from my father. The first jab was friendly. They escalated based on the time it took you to remember. It was a lesson you learned quickly. One hand was used for the fork, the other hand rested on your lap, until and unless, you required its use for cutting your meat, one piece at a time. Precisely that meant, fork in left hand, knife in right, cut, do not saw, one piece of meat, knife down, fork transferred back to right hand to eat the now cut piece of meat. Never, ever, did you spear your food. Cutting up everything on your plate at one time in a crisscross slash fashion was forbidden.

Belching at the table? Well, I could not even begin to imagine such a thing. We were sure that should a burp escape by some horrific accident, the perpetrator would be banished and forbidden from returning to the table for the rest of time. Outsiders could say many things about our family; sullen, secret, joyless and fearful, but we knew how to eat properly in public or private.

Casual banter at our dinner table did not take place. We sat down, food was served, we ate, cleaned our plates, and when finished, asked to be excused. Concentrating on good table manners gave my siblings and me something to occupy our minds until the meal was finished. Nicky and I in particular had become proficient in gauging my father's moods. And in the close proximity of our dinner table, it was a necessary skill. Being quiet and obedient was the surest route to take, short of not being there at all. My father did not shout and rage all the time, but there was an ever present and unceasing simmer beneath the surface of his moods that we all feared. Like an animal that sniffs the air for the approaching storm, Nicky and I kept our noses up for signs and signals, ready to make a hasty retreat away from flying debris.

When I remember Linda and our friendship, I remember her warm, friendly mother who treated me with kindness and caring. That kindness helped to create a time of grand adventure for me. Linda and I planned a day of shopping. Normally, my shopping meant a bike ride straight down Frazho Road to Gratiot and into Kresge's Dimestore. I hardly ever bought anything due to a lack of money, but it was a fun day because my friends and I felt grown up making the trek by ourselves. But this shopping trip was to be a ride on a Greyhound Bus. It meant putting money in the box as you stepped on the bus. Clink, in went the change and you walked the aisle to take a seat. We dressed up for the event. I wore borrowed clothes from Linda's closet. I wore a spring dress coat, navy blue that was an extra from Linda's closet. It was beautiful. I owned one coat, neither navy blue nor beautiful. We each carried a small purse, mine also borrowed.

Linda's mother watched as we boarded the bus and took our seats. It was surreal and fabulous. We sat tall, straight, and important, even though when we sat back, our feet never touched the floor. We spent the afternoon going from store to store just looking. Hudson's Department Store had more than one floor and shoppers could take the elevator or ride the escalator. We did both. I saw things that I had only seen in the Sears Catalog. I knew I would never own such splendor, but it was magical to be there and walk up and down the aisles pretending that someday I might own something from this grand store.

Before boarding the bus to go back home, we sat at the counter of a Sanders Ice Cream Shop and ordered a hot fudge sundae. The clerk set before me a beautiful mound of ice cream with soft, smooth, steaming hot fudge. It was my first taste of this particular hot fudge. I was speechless and instantly addicted to the sweet taste and velvety feel on my tongue with each spoonful carefully measured to ensure equal amounts of ice cream and hot fudge. It was nothing like the chocolate I had found hidden in the back of our refrigerator.

A later event was a humiliating one that, were it not for Linda's mother once again, would only bring shame and embarrassment at its remembering. It was a cool fall day, and I was happily on my way to Linda's house. My cheerfulness on this particular day was due to the recent acquisition of a brand new, hand-me-down, turquoise, faux leather jacket. Now finally, I had a fabulous jacket all my own to wear and show off. It was not new but it was new to me, and I loved it. And I was certain that I looked spectacular in that jacket. Linda and I had plans to do something outside on that day, which was great because I could wear my faux leather jacket the whole time.

I got to Linda's, rang the doorbell and waited. Her father came to the door. I had a fifty-fifty chance of this happening. Usually Linda answered the door and sometimes her mother, but once in a while on weekends, her father came to the door. I was not real fond of Linda's father. Actually, he frightened me. He never did or said anything to make me fear him, but he was tall, quiet and stern. That was enough. I did not have a good track record with adult males. In fact, they all scared me.

"Hi Mr. Kane," I said.

"Hello Christine. Come on in." He moved back to let me in. I squeezed in as far from Mr. Kane as I could and then waited.

"Linda is getting ready. She'll be out in a minute." His voice was low and quiet. Who talked like that? It sounded sinister to me. I imagined the head of the Creature from the Black Lagoon on Mr. Kane's shoulders. I watched him warily as he closed the door.

Mr. Kane did not tell me to go back to Linda' room, so I stood silently in the kitchen. It was cold and I moved closer to the small heating vent that went up from the floor and midway to the ceiling. I started to smell something funny. Linda's father turned, sniffed and moved me from the heater. There, on the louvers of the heater, was most of the back of my turquoise faux leather jacket. Tears welled up in my eyes, and I squeezed them back. They were tears for my jacket that was now ruined and tears because I had done a terrible thing to the heater.

Linda's father gave me a look that I had seen many times on the faces of adults. He was angry and only his Rosenbush manners kept his anger from boiling over on me. Linda's mother immediately took hold of me to see if I was burned and made soothing sounds to let me know it was okay, that it could be fixed. She even tried to see if my jacket could be saved, which was not to be.

I will never forget Mrs. Kane's kindness and compassion. I can still see her smile and hear her laugh. In my young world, kind and gentle adults were rare. Linda's mother had a laugh and a smile that made me feel safe and warm.

CHAPTER FOURTEEN

Shay Lake was our family get away, our cabin in the woods, a place to bond and frolic in the quiet of nature. Shay Lake was a small lake just outside Kingston, Michigan. Kingston was a small town located in the thumb area of the state and surrounded by other equally unknown small towns. My father acquired a piece of property in the area of Shay Lake at a time when a slick developer had make promises of developing the densely wooded area into a deluxe vacation spot. That grand vision never materialized. Still, we had a piece of vacation property.

Besides the lake, there was a large clubhouse, dirt roads and lots and lots of trees. My father's carpentry skills came in handy when it came time to build a cabin on our vacation land. It was a one room structure with a door at the front and a door facing the back, total dimensions of 26x20 foot. The cabin itself was primitive; but then it was in the middle of trees, brush, rocks and a narrow gravel two track lane that passed as a road. Around us there appeared a cabin or two. People built as they were able and with what was available.

Our cabin did not have a bathroom or running water. The outhouse was four walls, a wooden seat over a hole in the ground and smelled like an outhouse. I hated it both for its smell and that dark hole that seemed to never end. Given my history with horror movies, I was certain that something was waiting to reach up, grab me and pull me down into an abyss. A very smelly abyss. I preferred using the woods and taking my chances with spiders, mosquitos, poison ivy and even snakes. None of those dangers were strong enough to pull me through a wooden seat hole and bury me in feces.

The whole bathroom thing was a problem, but fresh water was not. My father had dug and tapped into a natural spring. The water was fresh, cold and crystal clear. I loved the way it tasted and enjoyed scooping it up in my hands to drink. There was no real yard, just weeds, dirt, rocks, and stumps. The cabin looked like a giant hand had reached from on high and plopped it down in one spot. We played in the road because it was the only clearing and the absence of traffic made it a safe place to play.

Now that my father had brought his mistress into our lives on an almost permanent basis, it was only natural that she and her children be included on trips to Shay Lake. One particular weekend we were a caravan on the way north for a fun-filled time away from the city. Two cars were needed to bring everyone. Even though my father's 1952 Ford was huge, it could not hold a wife, a mistress and seven children of various ages and sizes. In our car were my father, who drove, my mother, Nicky, myself, Shirley Ann and Michael. Following close behind were Milly, Danny, Janet and Teresa. Joe, Milly's actual husband, was noticeably absent, as usual.

Expressways and car air conditioning were things far into the future. Gratiot Avenue was the great highway to almost everywhere. Traveling was long, hot in the summers, and tedious. Michael, still a toddler, rode standing up in the front seat between my mother and father. The back seat was low and deep when you are a kid. We did not see much scenery. It was inevitable that some touching would occur. Nicky and I elbowed, punched and kicked. We did so silently and out of sight. There were no warnings or threats of consequences from the front seat if we did not behave. Our warnings came in the way of instant corporal punishment.

I was car sick on almost every trip so I made an effort to sleep as much as possible. Our car was a four door sedan with fabric seats that smelled of dust and stale cigarette smoke. The smells alone added to the nausea that hit me at the first turn of a key. My parents kept the car windows down for the ride and the coolness of it was a welcome relief. It felt good except when my parents smoked. The fresh wind swirling to the back seat carried the cigarette smoke with it. My nausea became accompanied by a headache. When we finally got to the cabin, we all jumped out screaming, as much from relief as from excitement at the prospect of swimming in the lake to cool off.

Shay Lake was the birthplace of the Creature from the Black Lagoon. I am absolutely certain of that fact and will defend it to my grave. The shoreline was a mound of rotting seaweed. As hard as I tried, there was no way to avoid stepping into the sun warmed slime to get out into the lake. Black muck sucked at my feet. I could feel myself being pulled into the Creature's lair. Then, just before his scale claws could grab me, I was in the sandy part of the lake. It was touch and go every time. But you were never completely safe in Shay Lake. Seaweed grew up and grabbed at your legs when you tried to swim.

Despite the danger of getting grabbed by the Creature and taken away to live in its deep sea cave home forever, we played in the water. Janet and I would play king of the hill in the water. With my brother, Nicky, perched on Danny's shoulders and I on Janet's, we fought it out. Danny and Janet were both bigger and sturdier than Nicky and me, so we always got to be on their shoulders. Janet never complained, and I liked being on top of the water, high above the Creature's grasp. As fun as that was, Janet would get tired so we had to get out and find other things to do.

Janet and Christine

Danny, fifteen years old now, had grown tall and I thought, movie star handsome. He became the object of my unrequited love and devotion from afar. Because it was necessary to hide my true feelings, I had to be satisfied with adoring him in doleful looks, attempts to be near when he was around and looking for ways to make myself useful to his every whim. One morning everyone was up and outside except Danny. He liked to sleep late.

Sleeping late in our house was never an option. Soon after my father was up and awake, we were up and awake. So it was noteworthy that Danny was sleeping so late into the morning. I expected my father to go in there and yell for Danny to get up. But as we were learning, my father had different rules for his mistress and her children. The more tolerant he became with Milly and her children, the more rigid, angry, and intolerant he became with my mother and his own children. His smiles and good nature seemed to be spent in their direction, leaving nothing for us. There was a price for adultery and the cost was exacted from his children and wife. Milly and her children experienced grace and tolerance. Our plate was served up with a rage and rigidity that grew daily.

Since my father did not go in the cabin and demand that Danny "get his ass out of bed" as he often did for Nicky and me, I contented myself with watching through the window at a slumbering Danny. As I longingly stared, I noticed his wristwatch lying on the table. Uh-ah, I thought. I could help him out and wind his watch while he was still sleeping. Putting myself in stealth mode, I snuck into the cabin, grabbed the watch and went outside. Sneaking around the back of the cabin where no one would see me perform this good deed, I hunched down and proceeded to wind the watch. And wind, and wind, and wind. Finally the little stem would not move anymore. There. I gave it one more twist for good measure. I casually walked back into the cabin and put the watch back on the table. I went outside smiling.

I imagined Danny coming outside declaring, "Hey, who wound my watch? Thanks! I was hoping someone would do that for me." And I would, of course, march center front and gracefully tell him, "You're welcome. It was nothing," looking humble and smart at the same time.

A short time later Danny was up. Dressed and outside, I heard him say to his mother, "My watch stopped. I think it's broken. I wonder what happened." Not for the first or last time in my life, I had the right to remain silent, and I availed myself of that right.

Boredom set in quickly on the weekends at Shay Lake. One activity that my sister and I enjoyed was pretending to drive the huge Ford. Teresa and Shirley Ann were inseparable by now, so the three of us would get in my father's car and take a trip somewhere, without ever moving of course. I was the sole driver because I was older and I made my sister and Teresa both passengers. They never argued so I took that as agreeing with me. Shirley Ann and Teresa sank into the back seat and sat quietly. They were good passengers.

Steering wheels then were as round and as big as barrel tops. It was easy to get a tight grip in order to make the big turns. It took both my arms to reach out and encompass the steering wheel. The gear shift was on the right side of the steering wheel column and it was fun to shift as you went. I never touched the gas, clutch or brake, mainly because my feet did not reach that far. I occasionally shouted orders at the passengers in the back seat.

The vehicles had cigarette lighters located conveniently on the right of the steering wheel down by the radio. You pushed the round cylinder in and when it was hot, it popped out. The coils were bright red and searing hot. The car did not have to be running for the lighter to work, so I could enjoy pretending to smoke as I pretended to drive. I thought this made me appear grown up and highly intelligent. Being keenly observant, I had watched my parents steer, shift gears, push in the lighter, light a cigarette and drive without missing a beat. This impressed me and I tried to do the same in my pretend driving.

On this particular trip down the dirt road by our cabin, I was moving along smoothly on my way to destinations unknown. Traffic was clear. I reached down and pushed the cigarette lighter in as I had seen my parents do countless times. Seconds later it popped out. Usually I just ignored it from there but this time I decided to have a closer look. Leaving my driving for the moment, I pulled the lighter out and turned the hot end to my face so I could closely inspect the coils. It was perfectly round with bright red little coils all in circles inside. I wondered just how hot those coils really got. I was not stupid. I knew better than to put my finger inside the little circle. But I wondered what would happen if I just touched the end to my leg. . .

In order to avoid having to answer questions about how the round burn got on my leg, I scrambled around and found a Band-Aid. The rest of the weekend was spent avoiding any situations in which my parents could see my leg and the perfectly round burn with tiny coil circles.

CHAPTER FIFTEEN

Aside from the weekly outings to the movies and occasional trips to Shay Lake, growing up poor meant limitations in what you did for entertainment, where you went, and who your friends were. As the neighborhood grew, it brought new people. The new families were not merely strangers, they were strange. It seemed the new people taking up residence in brand new homes being built around our older homes most certainly had to be very rich. Who else could actually buy a house already built? My father had built the house we lived in, so to imagine some stranger building your house was a mystery indeed. The newcomers made my small world bigger and a little frightening. Still, I bravely ventured forth beyond Firwood, the dirt road that bordered our house. This is how I met Pamela, who would become my best childhood friend. If you saw Pamela, you saw Christine. If you saw Christine, not far away, you would see Pamela. We played together, ran the roads and sidewalks together, ate dinners at each other's houses as often as our mothers could be persuaded, giggled and we fought as only bonded friends can do, ever remaining as close as sisters. As an adult, I came to realize we could not have been more different. Pam had dark brown hair and brown eyes; I was blond and blue-eyed. I was loud, Pam was steady. I was timid, to the point of fearful. Pam was bold, often acting as my protector. She was someone I trusted and loved for her loyalty and caring.

Pamela and Christine, 1958

Sleepovers were not something that we did often. My bedroom was small, hot and stuffy, and my bed was tiny, so there was not much to offer in the way of enticements to my house for a sleepover. And, I regularly wet my bed. That was not the type of information I wanted to get out. This was another reason my friends were not invited to sleep over.

One summer afternoon, Pam invited me to spend the night with her. I can only assume that I accepted in a momentary lapse of sanity because wetting my bed was not confined to my bed exclusively. My mother said yes, Pam's mother said yes, and Pam and I went into a frenzy of planning for the adventure. Dragging the necessary pajamas and clean underwear, I went to Pam's house. I ate dinner with her family, played outside until dark and then came in to get ready for bed. Only then, as it became dark did I begin to panic that I might wet Pam's bed. No, I told myself, it will not happen. Please, I silently begged, do not let it happen.

We went to bed, giggled and talked until Pam's mother gave us a final warning. Only then did we drift off to sleep. Very early in the morning I woke up to the familiar feeling of cold, wet sheets under me. I froze in shame and panic. I did not move. I felt tears stinging my eyes. I clenched my jaw and willed the tears away. Pam woke up and without a word we both worked to clean up the sheets. I snuck into the bathroom where I put on my dry things and then went to breakfast.

In the kitchen, Pam quietly and casually said, "Mom, I wet my bed last night. The sheets need washing."

"Oh? You did?" her mother said, as quietly.

I stood staring at the floor, wishing I could be anywhere but here and biting back tears of shame and embarrassment.

"Yea. Will you change them?" Pam said.

"Of course. What do you girls want for breakfast?"

That was the end of it. Pam's mother knew exactly what had happened and which one of us had wet Pam's bed but she said nothing. Not a word was said about it that day or any other day. For the rest of the day we played, laughed, argued, made up and ran until dark. Today we might say, she had my back, but then in my world, no such language existed to describe the vigilant, confident friend Pam was and remained throughout our childhood.

Boys came into our world just about the time we entered fourth grade; Chuck and Jimmy, to be precise. Awkward and shy, we did not consider that two of us might be a couple. In fact, for that brief summer we were just four kids playing in the warm sun of Michigan. We ran barefoot in the grass and as summer progressed, we made our way barefoot onto the gravel roads. It took a part of spring and into summer each year to toughen up bare feet, but it was necessary. Extra footwear was not a priority expense to my parents and shoes in the summertime were an encumbrance. It simply did not occur to us to wear shoes in the warm weather of summer.

Pam and I had spent the day doing whatever it was that at that moment in time seemed a good thing to do. Later in the afternoon, Chuck and Jimmy arrived riding on their slick Schwinn bicycles. They rode into the back yard, pushed on the peddle brakes hard enough for the back tire to skid in a devil-may-care way, hopped off and let the bikes fall. Putting the kickstand down was not cool. As the bikes fell to the ground both boys swaggered over to the picnic table where we sat. Taking the time to push down a kickstand ruined the swagger effect.

"Hi," said Chuck.

"Hi," Pam and I said in unison.

"Hi," said Jimmy.

Silence.

That was the extent of our conversation. The lull proved my undoing.

Every yard in my corner of the neighborhood had stuff; wooden swing sets in various stages of disrepair, wooden sheds in need of repair, slides, an occasional rabbit cage, dog pens, some occupied, some empty and full of weeds, and brick built barbeques, which seldom saw actual barbequing. Ours, also built by my father, was used for fires to sit by long into summer nights, roasting marsh-mallows on wooden sticks hastily cut from a tree, and for watching sparks fly upward into the nighttime sky. And on this particular day in my backyard, there stood one old, rusty, empty 50-gallon drum. Normally it was half full of rain water. But today, and to my soon to be most mortifying moment, it was empty.

Because nature and small children abhor a vacuum, I suggested in a moment of genius that we tip the drum over and ride on it. If I had shut my mouth at that point, the day would undoubtedly have ended with Pam and me excitedly sharing a 'date' with two neigh-borhood boys. But instead, I suggested we take turns hopping on and rolling the barrel with bare feet. I insisted on taking the first turn because it was my yard and my barrel. No one objected. Over the drum went and up I jumped, planted my bare feet and began what I was certain would be a feat compared only to the glamorous circus performers on the high wires.

Quickly loosing footing, arms flaying wildly in a useless attempt at graceful balance, I flew backwards off the drum, landing with a thunder like thud flat on my back. The wind knocked fully and completely out of my lungs, I could not suck in any air. The image is seared in my brain. My arms went out, fingers clawing at the dirt in panic, legs thumping up and down, my feet digging franti-cally into the soft grass while trying to get a breath. Three people stood bent over me, three sets of eyes staring, mouths gaping in horror at my predicament. Although in retrospect, it was probably more at my strange thrashing display rather than any alarm over whether or not I was dying, which I was certain was my fate on that sunny afternoon that had started out so grandly.

I did not die. With as much dignity as one can muster after pawing on the ground and making strange, guttural sounds, I got up and brushed myself off. No one said a word. This ended our glorious and romantic afternoon. To her credit and kindness, Pam never mentioned the incident again. She was a true friend.

Not long after that summer, the unthinkable happened. Pamela and her family moved away from the neighborhood. This tragedy was made endurable only by my frequent summer visits. Pamela's new house was built on a canal coming off the St Clair River. We spent hot summer days swimming and swinging out over the canal on a tire swing and dropping into the cool water. It was where I learned to swim. It was embarrassing to be the only kid there with a life-jacket on, and so I simply learned to swim.

Those summer visits sealed my love of reading. Pamela and her sister had a collection of Nancy Drew Mysteries. She and I spent many summer afternoons lying around her room reading and not talking. Those summers remain some of the best of my childhood.

CHAPTER SIXTEEN

Christmas time at our house was magical for me. A couple of weeks before Christmas we went with my father to a Christmas tree lot. My father, Nicky, and I piled in our car and headed to Gratiot Avenue where several parking lots had been marked off and lights strung around the perimeter to better showcase the freshly cut trees. At least they had been fresh in or around November when they were cut in northern Michigan, loaded onto trucks, processed, and began the long ride to our city. To us, they were green and smelled like Christmas. My father led us up and down the rows of trees, carefully examining one and then another. Occasionally he would reach among the stacks of trees, drag one into the middle of a makeshift path in the snow covered ground to better examine it as a possibility. Thump! He slammed its trunk on the ground to shake off collected snow and inspect branches for what he called bald spots. One such imperfection was acceptable. Once home, dried out, and brought into the house, the bald spot was pointed to a corner of the living room, nicely hidden from view. A crooked trunk was no problem. More Christmases than not, our tree had a piece of string attached to the tree trunk, tied to a thumbtack that was then hammered into the wall.

Once a tree was decided on, paid for and tied to the top of our car, we headed back home, satisfied that we had once again purchased the perfect tree. Only when it dried out and all the branches relaxed, did the flaws become obvious. We did not care. My father put the tree firmly in its stand and added water. My mother then opened the boxes of decorations brought down from the small attic. The attic had decreased in size once a large portion of the space had been designated as our bedrooms. The remaining space was used as storage. My father was the only one I can remember ever going up into the attic, especially after one particular incident.

My mother was serving dinner at our kitchen table. Shirley Ann, still a baby, sat in her high chair. My father for some reason had crawled into the attic while we all sat around the table eating dinner. Without warning, my father's entire leg, up to the hip, came through the ceiling drywall and hung suspended over the table and our dinner. His leg hung like some inanimate object meant as a decoration. Nicky and I stared speechless, mouths open. My sister began to cry.

My mother screamed and kept repeating, "Joe! Joe!"

My father shouted without pause, "Shut up, Shirley! Shut up, Shirley!"

I believe an occasional expletive made its way into my father's continued shouts. I remained silent and motionless. I knew better than to make a sound in an emergency situation. Past history had taught me silence is not only golden, but safer as well. You do not get slapped for being silent.

My mother stopped screaming. My father's leg juggled and moved back and forth in a motion meant to dislodge his appendage from the ceiling drywall. The leg slowly rose up to the ceiling and disappeared from view. My father peered down through the jagged hole to survey the damage. He did not speak. Dust and debris lay scattered on the table. My father made his way down from the attic and stepped into the kitchen where he too looked up at the new hole. It was a very funny situation, but even as young children we had learned that laughter at the wrong time was not tolerated. Once again, silence was our best option. My father remained angry, my mother shaken, and we all went on with the day.

My parents strung lights on the Christmas tree, carefully avoiding the string now securely attached to the wall. After much time was spent untangling the light strands, checking for burned out bulbs, and replacing bad ones, the lights were hung. Our lights were multi-colored and large. They sparkled and made reflections on the wall. My brother and I were allowed to hang the bulbs and string the garland. Finally my favorite part came, putting the tinsel on the branches. It was so light and feathery; the slightest bit of air made it sway and shimmer. I loved the tinsel, and our tree was loaded with it every year. Lastly my mother put a sheet under the tree, wrapping it all around the stand.

Soon after the tree was up and decorated, it was time to decorate the windows. For this my mother got out the Christmas stencils, sponges and pink Glass Wax. The stencils were scotch taped to our living room windows; the sponges dipped into bowls of Glass Wax and dabbed onto the windows now covered with stencils. We put food coloring in the bowls of Glass Wax. Santa got a red suit, trees were green, and bells could be blue or any combination of colors we chose. It was all very festive and as much a tradition at Christmas as was our tree.

As a carpenter my father's work was sporadic during winter months, and the 1950s was a difficult time for laborers. But for me that was the last thing on my mind during the holidays. I spent considerable time going through the SEARS catalog, marking toys, bending pages and imagining opening the brightly wrapped packages on Christmas morning. Money or lack of it never entered my mind. As an adult, I marveled that my parents did what they did with as little as there was to go around. We were never disappointed on Christmas mornings. We came down the stairs to find multiple packages under the tree, all of them wrapped in colorful paper. Nicky was in charge of reading name tags and handing out the boxes. It was that hierarchy thing again. Each of us received the most coveted item on our list. One year I opened a pair of white ice-skates. No more hand-me-downs. No more wearing my brother's old brown skates. I had my very own. Those ice skates began my career as a graceful, world-famous figure skater.

Our front yard was large. There was one acre of land and our house and garage sat back a distance from the road, making the front yard spacious. Other than a tall elm tree, it was wide open. In the winter months, my father would fill enough space on the ground with water to create a sizeable ice pond for us to play on. I loved it best when there was no one but me on the makeshift skating rink and I could skate to my heart's content. Round and round I skated, arms flung wide, sometimes one leg kicked back high in the air and occasionally daring to skate backwards. It was glorious. In my mind, the crowds gathered to watch my artful skills and to applaud with amazement at my graceful movements after which I would bow in modesty to my adoring fans. I loved that time; skating all alone on the small frozen pond letting my imagination take me to wonderful and faraway places.

One year at Christmas, my big gift was a walking doll. This particular type of doll was popular at the time. It was two feet tall and had dark hair, or what passed for hair. After weeks of combing, curling and brushing, bald spots appeared. The doll was tall and stiff as you would expect with a hard plastic torso and limbs the same. The walking part came when you grabbed one arm and pulled forward, after pointing one leg slightly forward. The knees did not bend so it was awkward and she did not sit very well. I was happy with her anyway.

The most fantastic gift of all was my very own wristwatch. One Christmas morning, I found a tiny package wrapped and marked for me. When I opened the box there was the most beautiful, exquisite watch I had ever seen. The watch face was tiny and rectangular. It had a pearl face with gold numbers and tiny gold hands. An even tinier gold second hand circled quickly around. The straps were two black braided strands held together at the clasps. It took my breath away. I loved that watch and wore it every day until I lost it.

It was not like I had numerous items to keep track of and it got lost in the vast array of personal possessions. No, I just lost the thing. My first reaction was panic, fearing the retribution of my father for being so careless with a valuable item. I kept my mouth shut for weeks. I could not sleep and began to think it preferable that Dracula should just finish me off one night or the Green Slime should dissolve me. This way my parents would be so sorry at losing me, they would forget about the missing watch. Neither of those things happened. We did not live near a body of water so I could forget about the Creature from the Black Lagoon coming for me. I was stuck. I needed a plan.

The plan had to be one completely devoid of any actual verbal confession or face to face admission. Confrontations were a no-no in our house. There was only room for one emotional being in the house, and my father had that sewed up tight. To say that I was terrified of my father, his temper, his lack of compassion and his bullying nature does not adequately describe my feelings as a child growing up in that house. The rules of order were resolute: shut-up, do not ever speak up, never disagree, and keep out of the line of fire. My father was the only one armed in our house.

After suffering in silence and fear for what seemed an eternity, I came up with a plan. I would write my father a letter confessing all and promising to pay him back for the watch. The letter had to be read when I was out of reach, so I stuffed it in his lunch pail before he went to work and wrapped up a dollar bill with the letter. The money was a first payment with a promise to pay more for the lost item. I cannot recall where the dollar bill came from. I could have stolen it. That era must have encompassed my bandit days. For a while I was a pretty good thief, taking a dollar here and a dollar there, from a wallet left out or money on a counter top. I stopped when an adult or two made suspicious remarks about money that had gone missing.

My father came home from work the day of the letter and called me to have a talk. Heart thumping, I stood awaiting my imminent doom.

Instead, he was kind. "I'm not mad at you," he said as he hugged me. I still cried but am not certain if it was out of fear, relief or happiness at being hugged. "Don't be silly about paying for the watch."

I stayed silent, afraid of what would be next.

"Why didn't you just come to me and tell me what happened?" His voice was soft.

Silent as usual, I was remembering temper tantrums whenever he was crossed, received news not to his liking or had eruptions of rage for no reason. I was no idiot. I had learned long ago in my young life the safety of silence. But, he wondered, where had I gotten the dollar? I do not remember how I explained the dollar bill stuffed in his lunch pail. But I am certain that stealing was not mentioned.

CHAPTER SEVENTEEN

In 1959 a group of people from Michigan went to Alaska as pioneers to settle in what was called the New Frontier. On March 5th of that year, a caravan of people from my home state of Michigan went lock, stock, and barrel leaving their homes and kin determined to begin a new life. That was noteworthy and exciting. But a much more exciting event was my television debut. Well, my almost television debut.

I was in Mr. Baker's fifth grade class in 1959 at Alwood Elementary School. As part of our social studies and because it was the big story of the day, our class followed the stories of this brave group of people as they prepared to begin moving out of Michigan. In 1849 the first migration to Alaska was for gold. They were referred to as the 49ers, so it made sense to me that the group following just over a century later was to be known as the 59ers. The new group went to homestead and claim free land. Being ten years old I am not absolute on all the finer facts but I do remember events that took place in Mr. Baker's fifth grade social studies.

Mr. Baker was a tall, bald, slightly overweight, and kind gentleman who wore a white shirt and tie every day. But at my school every teacher dressed up so this fact did not make him stand out.

He also wore glasses with black frames as did several of my elementary teachers. I liked the way wearing glasses made you look smart and often wished I could wear them myself. Occasionally I would squint and blink furiously around my mother, hoping she would decide I needed glasses and run me off to the eye doctor. It never worked.

Our class was so caught up in the drama and romance of the 59ers we sang a song to honor the pioneers. It was a lively song with catchy lyrics, *Alaska the New Frontier*. I do not remember the entire song but I do recall practicing the song every day as part of our music class time. Not surprisingly, we were so talented that a local television station heard about us and invited Mr. Baker's fifth grade class to come on television to perform. The show was a live, morning talk show in black and white and hosted by Harry Jarkey. It was unbelievable to me that I was going to be on television. What a great opportunity. Who knew where it could lead.

We practiced until we hated that song but then we practiced some more. In order to look presentable for television, all the girls were instructed to wear a short-sleeved white blouse, with a small collar and a black or navy blue skirt. Along with my blouse and skirt my mother bought me my first pair of nylon stockings. Pantyhose were as yet unheard of. The stockings, as they were called, came two in a package, one for each leg, beige or some other non-descript color, with black seams up the back.

Seamless stockings were not yet around. When they did arrive sometime when I was in junior high, I thought they were a waste. How would anyone know you had stockings on if there were no seams running up the back? But for my first foray into stockings, there were black slightly raised, soft lines straight up the back. If took time and effort to keep the line straight each time you put on a stocking. It required twisting and turning backwards to make sure the dark seam made a straight line up my leg. It was not easy to do, and required several attempts. Keeping the seams straight was an acquired skill. The stockings did not stay up by themselves, so my mother bought me my first garter belt. It was white cotton with small zigzag stitching meant to make it look fancy. Four garters, two in front and two in back, hung at the end of about six inches of wide elastic which secured the stockings. Occasionally a garter would come undone. This brought a trip to the bathroom to re-attach.

Stockings were not stretchy so sitting for any length of time resulted in a large bubble at the knee when you stood up. And that prompted another quick trip to unhook the garter, hike the stocking up tighter and reattach it. By day's end, depending on how much sitting, kneeling or bending you had done, there could be a large portion of stocking folded and hooked into the garter. All in all, it was a good system. I liked wearing stockings because it made me feel grown-up and very wise. This made up for not being able to wear glasses.

The boys in our class were all instructed to wear white long-sleeved shirts with cuffs and black or navy dress pants. That was boring, I thought. Girls were much more fortunate when it came to clothes because we had choices. Due to the severe lack of money in my family, new clothes were limited for me but there were other clothing sources.

Occasionally a bag of clothing appeared from some unknown source. One summer I found a black wool skirt with multi-colored threads dotting out and up. It was too big, but that was of no concern to me. I got out my mother's Singer Sewing machine and ran a straight line of stitching up each side until it fit. Straight up and down and too long, it hung somewhere between my knees and ankles. I did not yet know how to hem so the skirt remained too long for my body. I proudly wore it to school with my seamed stockings. This became a challenge only when recess came around.

When the weather was warm enough, we played baseball during recess on the playground. Although our school did not require uniforms, it did not allow pants or shorts for girls. Dresses or skirts only. That rule did not stop me from playing baseball. One hot afternoon during a fierce game of baseball I came up to bat. I was a good hitter. After a solid base hit, I ran to first base in my black wool, too long skirt with my seamed stockings, tripping and jerking my way to first base. Gravel and sand came up and tore my stockings. No problem. I went home and sewed up the tears with brown thread to match the seams. The result was dark squiggly lines in various places along my legs resembling some new and strange disease.

The television appearance was approaching and our class was practiced to near perfection for our debut. I had performed in my mother's big dresser mirror just the right way to smile so I would appear humble and stunning at the same time. I was convinced my efforts would pay off. The day before our appearance I woke up feeling queasy and light-headed. I knew better than to say I felt sick. I convinced myself it would go away if I stayed quiet and so off to school I went. The feeling got worse as the day wore on and by early afternoon I sat with my head down on my desk biting back nausea, keeping my eyes closed so the room would stop spinning.

Eventually, Mr. Baker noticed me and walked over to my desk. "Christine, are you not feeling well?"

I lifted my head up and saw two of Mr. Baker but said, "No. I feel okay."

Mr. Baker put the back of his hand to my forehead to check my temperature, which was the only sure-fire method for evaluating a fever, and determining that I did indeed have an elevated temperature, sent me home.

The next morning at 9:00 a.m., I was flat on my back on our gray couch, a bucket nearby for my repeated and frenzied vomiting, watching my class on the Harry Jarkey Show sing *Alaska the New Frontier* without me. My new clothes lay in a chair nearby. A budding career snatched from my grasp before it had begun.

That same year something happened to convince me that God did not want me to become famous or to wear new clothes. I concluded that God was working on my pride issues but thought His methods were not the best. Easter was approaching which, of course, meant great amounts of candy but also a church service. We still did not attend as a family but it was imperative that we all go to Mass.

For this year's Mass outing, I got a new Easter outfit. All new, not one item was dug out of the hand-me-down bag. And it was snazzy, convincing me that everyone at church would see how beautiful I looked and stare in awe as I made my way regally down the aisle to the front pew. The front was chosen for the most visibility it offered me. The outfit consisted of a cream colored wool skirt and matching blazer with accompanying gold crest on the pocket, a white short-sleeved blouse with pearl buttons and, of course new stockings. The outfit hung majestically in my mother's closet as Sunday approached. Nothing was going to compare to putting on my new clothes on Easter morning. The coloring of Easter eggs, usually a high point of the season, paled in comparison.

Two days before, Easter disaster struck. My head ached and my whole body hurt. My mother determined that I had a fever by the same tried and true hand to the forehead. She called Dr. Rothman, our family doctor who was, I think, close to one hundred years old. He was tall, thin, had white hair and wore black rimmed glasses, solidifying my theory that all smart people wore black rimmed glasses. He came to the house to treat us whenever we were sick.

Dr. Rothman pushed my tongue down with the flat stick, shown his tiny light inside my mouth and said, "Hmmm." Then he stuck the tiny glass thermometer under my tongue and told me to keep my mouth closed. He listened to my chest with his icy cold stethoscope and said, "Hmmm." He pulled the thermometer out, shook it hard enough to crack his wrist, peered at the mercury line inside it and said, "Hmmm."

Finally he said to my mother who had been standing in the doorway of her bedroom watching his every move, "She has measles."

Was he kidding me? If I could have lifted my head off the pillow of my mother's bed, I would have told him to get out, but all I could manage to do was to turn over and hide my face deeper in the bed clothes. And so I spent Easter morning not in my stunning new outfit, the envy of all, but in a dark bedroom, shades shut tight against any glimmer of light.

It all seemed completely unfair to me. To make matters worse, I was too sick to eat my Easter candy. I concluded that God thought fame and new clothes were evil.

CHAPTER EIGHTEEN

Sometime following my eleventh birthday things changed dramatically for me. Nothing in my outward circumstances had changed. My father was still a ticking time bomb, my mother was sad every day, we all still lived waiting for the next explosion and its aftermath, and my father continued to court his mistress under our noses. Despite the hovering Tsunami, I knew things had changed for me because Danny appeared quite different to my young eyes.

He was no longer the chubby kid I saw every day. Instead, a young, very handsome man, six feet tall, with a swagger to his steps, now lived next door. My world once consisting of dolls, bicycles, and picking gravel out of my wounded knees, suddenly, and with a crash, ground to a halt. My search for a husband was over. I could now rest easy. He lived not two hundred feet from me. I had decided he was the one.

Danny, 16 Years Old

Unfortunately, a few minor obstacles were present. Danny was sixteen years old, five years my senior. He dated females his own age, possessed of curves and other attributes obviously absent from my immature body. He barely noticed me and when he did, it was as the skinny kid who played dolls with his sister. For a time these small things challenged me. Considerable thinking was spent in trying to work out the solution. It did not occur to me that this opportunity would slip by. I remained resolute. I watched and waited.

One night in bed as I mulled over my situation, an epiphany broke over me. Of course. How stupid I had been to not think of it. My ace in the hole. Prayer. I would simply put this all before God, sit back and wait. And that is just what I did every night for five years, 60 months, 240 weeks, 1680 days. My prayer was not, "make him want to marry me". Who wants that? No, I put my plan before God: Please keep him single until I am old enough. Just give me a fighting chance. I figured that was reasonable enough and God could not fault me for that. And if God thought my whole plan was a disastrous one, He never told me. But in the five years of praying and waiting, neither did I falter in my goal or change my mind.

It was during this time that I began to hone one of my greatest skills, stalking. Not ever having heard the term before, it nonetheless became my special art form. I am one of those who helped to perfect the particular skill of stalking. It will someday be credited to me as using this for good, which was, of course, my only aim.

Living next door to my future husband offered untold opportunities to keep watch over the man earmarked for me. There were myriad vantage points from which to observe and I marked them all. When young teen friends arrived in cars, I sat on my porch and watched. Leaving to pick up a date, tall, slick and dressed up, my gaze followed his departure. When the Pechacek house or backyard became alive with Danny's counterparts, my attic bedroom window afforded me a front row seat. Sitting at the top of the wooden steps, window open, gave me the perfect view. There were never any extraordinary events, but still I sat motionless and stared. I doubt I was detected but even if one set of eyes had noticed me, who cared that a skinny kid next door watched the neighbors. If anything, I was probably dismissed as some weirdo. I did not care.

A secret reconnaissance mission took place anytime I could get inside the Pechacek house.

This move I managed on an almost daily basis. Lucky for me, Danny had two sisters. Even though Janet was three years my senior and in a different circle of friends, I found ways to infiltrate their activities. In the beginning, Janet still played with dolls, a pastime I also enjoyed. The best part with the dolls connection was the fact that Janet's dolls were new and had store-bought clothes. This worked out for me on two levels. I maneuvered myself into the Pechacek house at will to observe my future husband, and I got to play with some cool dolls. Life certainly did throw some great things my way every once in a while. So for a time, I moved freely about inside the fortress watching and taking note of details. Danny's bedroom consisted of one neat twin bed, a small dresser, one desk with a small lamp and one window. The window was important to note.

The doll playing worked well until Janet moved beyond dolls to boys. First of all, I did not care for boys in general. All the boys my age were not worth noticing; and besides, I was already spoken for, even if my intended was not yet aware of this fact. Patience. I needed to have great patience. In the meantime, I stuck to my post.

Saturday nights for Danny meant either going on a date or to a party with friends. I am certain this included finding girls for dates. My mind did not go beyond that. What lurked in the thoughts of a healthy sixteen or seventeen year old was yet unknown to my young mind. That was a good thing. I knew this ritual well because early Saturday evenings I would be at one of my prime posts, either our front porch or my bedroom window waiting and watching. Dressed and groomed slick as dynamite, he came out his front door, cigarette in hand, and swaggered to his 1957 Chevy Convertible. The engine roared, and he was gone. In my mind, I was on the seat next to Danny. As he drove down Frazho Road on his way to places that I did not yet imagine existed, I was then free to leave my post. Late into the night, if I was lucky, the noise of the engine would awaken me in time to see him come home and go inside. Then it was back to bed for me. Mission accomplished. I tucked myself in and could then rest peacefully.

To my knowledge, Danny never rose before noon on Sunday morning. Not wanting to miss a sighting, I was out the door quietly but quickly. Crossing the yards casually, I sat down on the ground directly under his bedroom window. Summer time meant it would be open. Perched silently, I could sit for extended periods of time, waiting for some sound of life. I am not sure what I expected to hear or see. But sometimes my waiting was rewarded with a voice.

"OK! Ok, I'm up." No movement. Minutes passed.

"DANNY!" There was no mistaking his mother's call. Milly's tone and pitch had the ability to pierce armor. Your ears echoed in its aftermath. Unfortunately for her and those forced to endure its repeated sound, Danny had some secret resistance to its power. Adding to this gift, or perhaps due to it, he was also spoiled and arrogant. At some point, however, even he tired of the call and stirred. After listening carefully for the sounds of rustling, bed linens moving, feet hitting the wooden floor and a yawn or two, I stealthily made my way back home.

Nicky, 1955

My brother, Nicky, and Danny had developed a camaraderie which I saw as another opportunity for me to get closer to Danny in various ways. Their friendship was often characterized by some risky behaviors. One summer afternoon, Nicky sat at the attic bedroom window waiting for Danny to come the back door of his house. After a short time Danny came out, letting the wooden screen door slam behind him as he headed the short distance to the small shed at the back of their property.

A sharp *ping* sounded and Danny grabbed his behind. He jerked his head towards our house and stared up to the window. There sat Nicky, BB gun in hand, with a wide grin on his face. Barely missing a step, Danny ran into the shed, grabbed his BB gun and aimed. What ensued was a short but furious BB gun battle. No eyes were shot out, and other than the initial smart sting to Danny's read end, no physical harm resulted from the foray. However, several shed window panes were not so lucky. The window in my bedroom became a casualty as well. It ended as quickly as it had begun. I cannot recall what consequences resulted for either of them; but suffice to say, there was never another BB gun battle on Frazho Road.

In order to keep communication open and ever ready between the two houses, my brother and Danny managed to connect a make shift two-way radio contraption. By holding down a button, you could call from house to house. This could not have been any better for me. Occasionally I would use the device to call Janet, knowing of course she would not answer. The radio was in Danny's bedroom. It was just a clever way for me to get him to talk to me. That ploy did not last long, however.

Danny, 1955

"Damn it. Stop calling here. I'm sleeping."

Oops, time to ditch that plan.

Never short of ideas, my next plan involved my Peeping Tom stage. One afternoon while all the Pechaceks were gone, Danny decided to entertain one of his many female friends at home. Once they were situated in the living room, I made my move. The front of the house had one entry door and a very large picture window, as did almost every house.

Most fortunate for me, the flower bed sat directly under the window and held one enormous green shrub, making it perfect for camouflage. With practiced stealth, I positioned myself for a clear view. Truth be told, hiding was probably not necessary. They were not looking out the window. A record was on the 45 RPM record player. Danny lay on the couch. She sat at his head, singing Brenda Lee's popular *Sweet Nothings* to him as he smiled. He pretended to swoon. I thought the whole thing looked silly. She could not sing. I knew this because of my vast experience in singing and my almost television debut on the Harry Jarkey Show. This particular female was average looking, and I knew whatever she imagined developing between the two of them was out of the question. He had pretty high standards. I also knew he was going to pick me one day anyway. But once again, I reminded myself to be patient. Besides, there was that age thing. I needed to get older. Becoming bored, I crawled out from the shrubbery and went home.

On another occasion when a female was in the house with Danny, the atmosphere was not so quiet and gentle. One of the females Danny was dating decided to come to his house in the middle of the night to make a surprise visit. She drove with friends from St. Louis to pop in for a visit. Unfortunately she decided to make this visit in his bed while his parents slept in another room. Alcohol was involved. Managing to sneak in undetected, she did not stay that way. Danny's mother woke up. Screaming ensued. A loud and colorful exchange followed, which was a plus, because it meant the next door neighbors got to watch and listen. I heard every word. Her friends drove off when the action started. After managing to calm his angry mother, who had thrown this female bodily out the front door onto her behind, Danny drove her back north. I thought Danny's mother handled the situation quite well all things considered. But even if I did not understand the concept of irony as of yet, I thought it strange that Milly should object to her son being in bed with a strange female.

Over the next four years, I witnessed the unusual, the humorous and the frightening, up close and personal. That such behavior over the succeeding years did not awaken me to a future of heartache and pain said volumes about my own miserable existence. It all somehow seemed normal.

CHAPTER NINETEEN

Sometime around eleven years old I started driving and by my twelfth birthday, I was a darn good driver. My father taught both my brother and me to drive in the family car, a 1954 Ford, standard transmission. At first it was just up and down the driveway, becoming accustomed to the clutch, shifting the gears, and remembering where all the gears were on the column. First gear, pull towards you and then down; second gear, out and away and all the way to the top; third gear, back down again. Got it. Reverse, pull towards you but go all the way back to the top. Neutral was in the middle of the column and loose.

Nicky and I were not the only pre-teens in our neighborhood to drive at a young age. It was a time when kids learned to drive as soon as your feet touched the pedals. My father did not particularly like to drive so he was more than willing to slide over when one of us asked to drive. It was inevitable that sooner or later there would be some consequence to this early illegal activity. Unfortunately, it happened to me first.

It was the summer of my parents' divorce. My father had gone off with the woman of his grand passion, leaving his family to sink or swim. What we did was sink. My father had left without a word of explanation to his children. He had just packed up and left with Milly to parts unknown. My mother remained at home to raise my siblings and me with no skills and little money. To support herself and her children she was able to find a small factory job. Her days were intense, exhausting and busy, leaving little time for any personal pleasure. And we were left largely on our own.

One particular Saturday my mother was gone with friends to parts unknown. Her Mercury was in the driveway, keys in the ignition, as usual. I was bored. At fourteen, I fancied myself grown-up, sophisticated and extra smart. No one else was home. Shirley Ann and Michael were with my mother. What to do. . .what to do. . .

In a flash of genius or a sudden psychotic break, it could have been either; I decided that I would drive my mother's car to the shopping center. I had no money to spend but driving the car to the shopping center would be the best part anyway. Since I did not want anyone to know what I was doing, I decided to go alone. I casually went out the front door, walked to the 1958 black and yellow Mercury, got in and started the engine. So far, so good. Very carefully backing out, I headed down Frazho Road to Gratiot Avenue on my way to the nearby shopping center. It was just two miles down the road with no stop signs or traffic lights along the way. Until, that is, I hit Gratiot. Gratiot Avenue was a main highway, two lanes in each direction, separated by a median and a traffic light. No problem. I had done traffic lights before while driving with one of my parents riding shotgun. Red—stop. Green—go. The yellow light made me nervous. I could never decide whether to speed up and go through the yellow light or go real slow and wait to see if the light turned yellow at which time I would slam on the brake. I was spared that dilemma on this particular trip.

When I got to Gratiot, the light was green. The shopping center was directly across Gratiot Avenue and an easy right hand turn into the parking lot. That was easy enough. I pulled into the discount store parking lot and because I was very sure of myself as a driver, I decided to park right up close alongside other parked cars. The rear of the lot had ample spaces but this would be much better. I could show off my advanced parking skills. Unfortunately, my depth perception was not quite as developed as I thought; and apparently not to the point of recognizing how much space the huge Mercury needed.

As I turned the Mercury into a spot I was confident was big enough, I heard *squeeek*. The sound of metal on metal. I looked out my driver's window at the rear bumper to see it scraping the side of another car. Not good. I could see no other alternative but to go out the same way I came in. I backed out. *Squeeekkk*. Heart pounding, near panic, and all my confidence gone, I drove back home. I cannot remember if the light was green or red. I just drove home, parked the car and sat in the house, using my time until my mother came home to form a plausible story as to how the paint on the side of her car had suddenly gotten scraped off. Nothing was jumping out at me. I decided to go with my usual defense. Silence. And if confronted with evidence, plead ignorance.

My mother eventually came home, and once again I availed myself of my right to remain silent. Later that afternoon two very tall policemen came to the door to inquire whether or not my mother had been at the shopping center earlier in the day. She assured them she had not and had been with friends for the day.

"Ma'am, witnesses observed your vehicle, the black and yellow Mercury parked in your driveway, leaving the scene after causing some damage to another parked vehicle," the tall policeman explained.

"Oh no, that's not possible Officer. The car has been parked right here all day, and I've been gone." My mother was very convincing, as happens when you tell the truth. Well, she believed it to be the truth.

Standing directly behind my mother, attempting to remain invisible from the eyes of the law, and practicing my most innocent face, I remained silent.

"Well, Ma'am, I do need to caution you that it can be unwise to leave your keys in the ignition," he said. "Someone could take the car without your knowledge." He was looking at me, but I did not break.

They left and I never told my mother of the little escapade. I decided not to give her more to worry about so soon after the divorce. The truth was, I decided if no one could point me out as the culprit, then I would keep my finger pointing out of it as well. The issue of the paint damage did not come up then or in any future conversations.

By the end of that summer I had left my mother and moved in with my father and his mistress. My decision to leave my mother brought pain to her soul from which she never recovered. She gave no response the day I told her of my decision, just put her head down, turned and walked away. She had watched her family, and her life erode bit by bit, powerless to stop the onslaught of destruction. I was one more piece sliding into the abyss. At fourteen years old, immature, and selfish, I could not fathom the darkness that engulfed my mother to see another part of her life, her soul, leave. I gave no thought to anything but myself. I was a child and perhaps that can explain my actions; but in my adult mind, it affords me little peace.

The move to live with my father brought no welcome from him and certainly none from his mistress. Just as it had been when my parents were together, I was more or less invisible. Teresa, Milly's youngest daughter was a part of our little fractured household as well. My father and Milly had moved to Mt. Clemens into a small rented ramshackle house, and set up less than blissful housekeeping. The beginning of their new life together was far from idyllic. Arguments followed by silence became the pattern of this new household. My father was often morose and withdrawn. Milly went from aloof to silent and pouting on a regular basis. It was to become a pattern that governed their lives and consequently mine and Teresa's as well.

I turned fifteen in January with little fanfare from anyone. The adults in our lives were so consumed with themselves, their lust, and the drama that surrounded it all that our birthdays faded into insignificance. It was noted by a card and birthday cake at best. The obligatory birthday song was sung, candles blown out and stilted smiles shared. Then it was over and we all returned to our own silence. By this time, I had been driving for three years. Not having a driver's license was a mere formality. My father would send me on the odd errand now and then. We lived in a small, out of the way area and traffic was scarce. One such errand turned interesting. It involved me and the police once again.

We had ordered pizza from a small mom and pop neighborhood store one Saturday afternoon. The order required picking up. My father told me to drive down to the store and pick up the pizza. Great. Their car at the time was a little blue Renault with a standard transmission. No problem. That it was a small car meant parking would be no problem. I had learned about parking before. I hopped in the car, wallet in hand with money to pay for the pizza, and off I went. The store parking lot was small and unpaved. There was just one other car parked in front. That was good for me. It gave me plenty of room to park. The Renault was half the size of the big Mercury monster. Confident and perky, I got out of the car and went inside the store. The small building was packed with stock, leaving little room to walk. One aisle led directly to the front where the check-out counter with register stood. Wallet in hand, I headed straight to the counter to give my name, pick up the pizza, pay and drive back home. Like so many days in my then short life, this would not go according to plan.

One man stood at the counter checking out, I assumed. A woman was behind the counter at the register, a young man stood off to her left and behind them both stood a taller man. He had a gun. The hand gun was pointed at the head of the woman in front of the register. I stopped and stood very still.

The man with the gun pointed it at me and said, "Put your money on the counter." I laughed. I am not sure why I thought he was joking, but I did.

The woman whose head was once again in the gun's aim said, "He's not joking."

I opened my wallet and poured out the small amount of money I had brought with me. My hands were shaking and my legs threatened to give out beneath me. There were several bills already on the counter, presumably from the one other customer. The woman emptied the cash register and put the money on the counter. The man with the gun grabbed up all the bills. Waving his gun, he told us to get into the cooler behind the counter at the back of the store. We all got in the cooler. Once he shut the door, we sat in silence. It seemed a very long time passed before anyone dared to move.

The woman spoke, "We'll wait a couple of minutes in here to be safe and make sure he's gone."

No one offered any other ideas. We all waited. Finally, she opened the cooler, stuck her head out cautiously to look around and motioned that the man was gone. We all filed out. The store clerk called the police. Waiting for the police, the three people started talking in hushed whispers. I said nothing.

The police came. After that things moved quickly and conversations returned to a normal level. The police kept new customers out of the store. Each of us was asked all the necessary questions: name, address, what did you observe, description of the man. Because I had arrived last and while the robbery was in progress, I had been the only one to see the thief's car. Having developed keen observational skills from my days of stalking Danny, I was able to give a clear and accurate description.

Finally the woman must have noticed that I was young and asked, "Do you want to call someone and let them know what happened?"

Feeling very grown-up and calm, I said, "Okay. Sure." I made it sound like being robbed at gun point and locked in a cooler while the bandit made his getaway was an everyday occurrence for me.

She handed me the phone and I dialed the number. My father answered.

"Daddy," was all I got out before a torrent of tears, sobs and choking sounds came from my chest. The woman quickly took the phone from me and told my father what had happened and that the police were there and no one had gotten hurt. After a minute, she handed the phone back to me. My sobs had quieted and I was no longer choking on each breath.

Putting the phone to my ear, I heard my father say, "Don't tell the police you drove there by yourself."

We did not get our pizza. And, I escaped the long arm of the law once again.

My driving experience had been wide and varied already. My rap sheet must have read: drove illegally, had fender-bender, escaped the law; drove illegally, held-up at gun point, escaped the law.

By the time I was eligible to take Driver's Education, I probably had as much experience as the instructor. While still living in Mt. Clemens, I had finished most of the book work for the driving course and had logged several hours of driving with an instructor. After the move to Emmett and I was enrolled in Memphis High School, I only had road hours to complete before I could take the test and get my license. The instructor, a high school language arts teacher, agreed to take me out on the road for the final hours required for completion. Highways in the thumb area of Michigan are long and monotonous with little traffic. It was just the instructor and I, a middle aged man, short, thin and arrogant.

"So, how do you like this area?" He smiled.

"It's okay. We haven't been here long." I assumed he was making small talk to pass the time.

"Do you have a boyfriend?" he asked, still smiling.

"I don't know very many people yet," I smiled back.

"Well, if you want to get to know anyone, let me know."

I could feel him staring at me. I was not frightened but he was creepy in an old man sort of way. He was irritating and silly as far as I was concerned. Besides, I had control of the wheel.

"No, I'll be fine," and kept my eyes on the road.

"I would be happy to show you around," he said. "You seem much older and more mature than most girls your age." Again, the smile.

We finished for the day. He passed me on the spot, telling me I was a far more experienced driver than of his other students. He signed my permit. I left, my father picked me up, and I never told anyone that the high school language arts teacher at my new school had hit on me. I found out later that he was already engaged in a sexual affair with another female student, not his first. This led me to believe that I was not all that fascinating, just new.

CHAPTER TWENTY

Summers meant I went to spend extended time with my mother. This particular summer I was just fifteen years old and considered myself very grown-up and worldly. Of course, I was neither of those things but, believing I was made life easier for me. Being grown up and sophisticated meant being capable of single handedly dealing with the insanity that had become my life. So it was more a matter of survival. Living with my father was both boring and tense at the same time. There was no father-daughter interaction. All of his physical and emotional energy was aimed at making Milly happy. It was a full time job, mostly because her happy scale criteria was arbitrary and changed daily, almost hour by hour. When Milly's scale hit low, things went from tense to dark for everyone in the house.

The move to Mt. Clemens had been fast and furious, happening right after my father received divorce papers from my mother. I had not made friends in this new neighborhood and until school started in the fall, it was not looking good for meeting new people. Teresa, Milly's eleven year old daughter, and I were not close. We had not even reached a friendship stage. Teresa was frightened and confused, which I saw as demanding and difficult. No one else recognized her pain either. As for me, it took all my energy to be the good daughter and adoring, selfless, silent step-daughter to the still mistress. All of us, my father, Teresa and myself, stepped carefully in order to ensure that Milly was happy, which made life pseudo-peaceful.

Getting the chance to go to Warren to visit my mother was a welcome change. Living with my mother was not much better but it was minus the manipulation, the rage sessions, and selfishness of my father and Milly. It was the difference between having the flu and having the chicken pox. Both made you sick, just different symptoms.

Visiting my mother meant a freedom I did not have at my father's house. He was a strict parent, which I did not mind. His type of parenting gave me boundaries. The strictness, however, was born more from it being easier to just say no to everything I wanted rather than to negotiate with Milly about fairness over what I could and could not do, and whether or not Teresa got the same privileges. No matter that she was four years younger, if Teresa could not do a thing or go somewhere, neither could Christine.

I still had friends in the old neighborhood who were within walking distance of my house on Frazho Road. I had lost contact with many of them during the divorce and the breaking up of the two families. It was a time when kids did not talk about divorce. Divorce held a stigma, and people tended to back away from you when it all became very public. Our situation was even more bizarre because of the infidelity. And not just infidelity, but open adultery and with a neighbor at that. It was high drama on Frazho Road. Still, being back in my old neighborhood gave me a sense of home, even as the house I grew up in had not.

My mother now belonged to a bowling league with new friends she had met through the factory job she acquired following the divorce. They bowled at Gateway Lanes on Groesbeck Highway, not far from our house. The group of women bowled the evening league because they all worked day jobs. I decided to tag along with my mother the weekend I was there. The din of the bowling alley hit me in the face the minute we walked through the doors.

There was laughter, the sound of balls rolling down the lanes, pins falling and what seemed like hundreds of voices all talking at once. The air had a continuous blue haze from the myriad cigarettes being lit, smoked or on the way to being stubbed out. My mother brightened when she got with her friends, laughing and talking with quick, short bursts of recent gossip. I did not see my mother smile often and laughing had become a rarity, so it was fun to go and get in on some happy time with her. I did not bowl and had no interest in learning or participating, but I enjoyed watching. Her team consisted of women her age, divorced and trying a little too hard to laugh and have a good time.

Occasionally one of the ladies would talk to me, asking me how I was, noticing how much I had grown and inquiring about things at my new home. But I was not all that interesting to women who wanted to be with friends and maybe meet men, so they soon went back to each other and bowling.

On this particular night I sat up and back from the lanes, watching people and listening to conversations. At the same time, I was taking note of any attractive males remotely near my age that may or may not notice my beautiful, poised self, sitting all alone. There were few. Most of the males stayed in the bar area, watching the women bowl and waiting for any stragglers who would come in for a drink after bowling. I had not been sitting alone very long when a very attractive male sauntered casually over to me.

"Hi. Mind if I sit down?"

Hell no, I thought to myself but out loud I said, "No, that's fine."

I was not averse to cursing. I had certainly heard enough at home. But I did not curse out loud, and never in front of my father. That was most definitely one of the rules in his house, no bad language, at least not by anyone other than himself. Although my father's actions were at odds with his verbal dictates to his children, I did learn the meaning of respect and appropriate behavior both in public and private. For this I am deeply grateful.

And sit down he did. He was 6'2", slender, blond, with the bluest eyes I had ever seen and a gorgeous face. He name was Glenn. I was not overly fond of the name Glenn, but I decided to overlook this because he was so drop dead gorgeous. Through our conversation I learned he was twenty-one years old. Clearly, he was too old for me, but I decided to overlook that as well. We talked. Glenn did not seem to notice and never inquired as to my age. I did not offer the information. He told me he had just stopped in for a beer, but when he saw me, he decided to stay and try to meet me. A line I am sure, but like a hungry fish seeing a big fat worm on the hook, I gulped the whole thing in one swallow. He then told me he was headed home and would I like to go for a ride.

Although I was young, my IQ was in the higher digits. I gracefully declined. Glenn decided to stay. We sat and talked under the watchful eye of my mother and her friends. The evening was over before I knew it.

"Can I have your phone number?" Glenn asked.

You bet you can, I said in my head. But aloud, "Sure. That would be okay." The self-assured sophistication oozed out of me. I wrote out my telephone number and handed him the piece of paper, thinking that would be the end of it even though I was sure my wit and charm had dazzled him beyond measure. I was equally certain he would get a clear head after he drove away and decide I was too young.

I was wrong. He called the next day and asked me out on a date. A real date. It would be my first. My father's rules were that I could not date until I was sixteen years old, no exceptions. But at my mother's, the rules were different and slack. Such is divorce. It can be like living in two parallel universes, one parent saying one thing, putting down rules but then you just hopped over to the other universe, and you can have different rules.

My mother said yes, I could go on this date with a man we did not know. My mother had met him briefly before we had left the bowling alley the night before but not enough to even remember his name. I am relatively certain I left out the part that Glenn was twenty-one years old.

He picked me up in a dark blue Pontiac, sleek and new, with white leather seats. Very nice. We went for ice cream, drove around talking for a while, and then we stopped at his parent's house to pick up something. He introduced me to his mother. She was a charming lady. We visited while Glenn gathered up some belong-ings. After the short visit, we left. As all dates then, it ended with Glenn parking in a cozy, quiet spot. We talked again and listened to the car radio. The song *House of the Rising Sun* came on, its slow melodious wave drifting through the car. Glenn told me it was his favorite song. I thought it a strange song, sad and dark but did not say so. Eventually, he put his arm over the back of the seat around my shoulders and drew me slowly to him. He kissed me very gently. It was slow, warm and soft. I was enjoying the moment immensely. After a few more very lovely of the same, alarm bells went off in my head. I was fifteen years old but not clueless, and I was old enough to know where Glenn was going with this. It was territory I had not traveled and terrain I had no intention of checking out then and there with him, no matter how good looking and charming. So I stopped the progression.

Laughing nervously, I said, "We need to go now."

Glenn stopped, pulled away to look at me and said, "Are you sure you want to go home now?"

I was not sure at that moment. I was enjoying the warmth of being held, the feel of his very soft lips and what they were doing to me, but I was also frightened. I was out of my depth and had not developed a meter for reading my own physical reaction to what was happening.

But I said, "Yes. I really am sure."

We left. He took me home, walked me to my door, kissed me one more time and drove away. That was the end of gorgeous, 6'2" blond, beautiful blue-eyed Glenn.

Or so I thought. He did call for me several times but my mother told him I did not live with her all the time and was not sure when I would be back. Glenn moved on.

Each time I hear *House of the Rising Sun*, I see those blue eyes, a delicious smile and hear his laugh. It would have been interesting to get to know Glenn over time. Maybe he was the gentleman he appeared that night in his car with the radio softly playing.

Living with chaos, I had learned several survival techniques. One was how to control my own self. I had no control over the crazy adults around me. I was not in charge of the decisions that affected my life, but I could be in charge of my own body and person. I decided who could get close and who would not. It was me that decided who would be allowed into the inner circle of my world, and who was regulated to the perimeters. It might seem bizarre but I believed it kept the "ME" safe. I kept a part of myself always outside the circle of my world where I could monitor the crazies. What I did not have was an inner library that I could refer to and measure against, in order to keep out those who would eventually destroy me. No system is perfect.

CHAPTER TWENTY ONE

Dating was not something at which I excelled. I could count in the very low numbers the boys I dated. Most would be a stretch to call the event a date. My career of dating began late by some standards; I was sixteen years old. My father was adamant about the proper age to begin dating. I could skirt around the age thing when I visited my mother and managed to sneak in a date or two at fifteen years old. But it was not easy. Very few of my friends dated much before sixteen so there was little in the way of plausible examples to point to as persuasion for my father to relent. I left it alone and waited it out.

There were also some house rules regarding dating. They were more like edicts from on high rather than house rules. My father made it very clear to me that:

- You will introduce a date prior to the date.
- The date will come to the door, enter the premises, and speak to me.
- Your date will bring you to the door at the end of the evening.
- You will be home by midnight. No exceptions. No excuses.

Because this was my first foray into dating, I was perfectly okay with all the rules. Also, I had no choice. And I knew there would be consequences should I ignore the rules.

Blind dates never end on a happy note. It just cannot happen. Friends mean well, but I do not understand what possesses a friend, someone who knows you to a certain degree and presumably more than casually, to match you up with a total stranger. Usually it is a stranger who could not get a date on his own and needed a go-between, and most assuredly it is someone your friend would not date themselves.

"He's really nice," Linda said. "He's a cousin of my boyfriend. I stared at her. Linda had been my friend since grade school.

"What does he look like?" I asked and feared the answer.

"He really is cute." I could hear the gentle pleading in her voice.

Against every instinct I possessed, I accepted. And he was cute. We went to the movies, which was a good thing since he did not say two words to me the entire evening. He was painfully shy. He kept his head lowered all evening, and I cannot remember ever looking at him eye to eye. Coupled with my own inexperience and complete lack of dating knowledge, we silently stumbled through the evening.

Apparently I was not a quick learner because another neighborhood girlfriend fixed me up with her brother. He was skinny and just my height. I preferred tall. I had to admit his looks were pleasant enough and he had a car. Our first and only date was to a drive-in movie. The movie had barely begun when his arms went out in a vice-like grip, grabbed my face and began what I am sure he believed was kissing. Admittedly my background in the art of kissing was limited, but this was like a mother cat attempting to lick the afterbirth off a newborn kitten. However small my experience in kissing was, I did not need a storehouse of knowledge to know this was not it. He was stricken off the list of possible future dates even into infinity.

Fix-ups or pity dates as I prefer to call them are inevitably headed toward, at best boredom and at worst, the how-can-I-get-out-of-this-fast syndrome. On any date I did attempt to head into the day or evening anticipating a positive outcome. Looking back I realize that my attitude was, more often than not, the pivotal turning point of any date. It never took long for me to decide whether or not this person was someone I wanted to be with and that showed in my every nuance.

One summer date while at my mother's visiting was with a young man who was at least sixteen years old. I knew this because he drove and owned his own car. John's car was a slick convertible. That was the biggest attraction for me. We arranged to go with another couple on a picnic. Being somewhat confident of my homemaking abilities, I offered to make fried chicken for our picnic. I had seen my mother fry chicken to perfection and it looked simple enough.

On the day of our date I bought chicken, cut it up in pieces, floured each piece and fried it in hot grease in my mother's sacrosanct cast-iron fry pan. Nothing could go wrong using the coveted pan. It even had the grease ready to go. My mother kept the grease in the pan after countless times of use, as did most of the moms I knew. Once the pot was cooled, it was put in a cold oven, grease and all, to await the next delectable dish.

The chicken fried, grease popping and snapping, and browned nicely. I was quite proud of my chicken frying skills and was already imagining the smiles and praise of my date. John arrived with his friend in tow, along with the friend's date. It was a beautiful day and because I did not get many chances to ride in a convertible, I suggested the top be put down. I was already envisioning my hair blowing in the breeze, smiling and resembling a television commercial I had seen.

We headed to a picnic spot some distance away. Traffic was heavy which made the drive stop and go. I had not anticipated sitting still in traffic in the hot sun with the top down. My hair was not softly blowing in the wind. It was plastered to my head with beads of sweat running down my neck and face. But, it was a convertible and we must have looked fashionable. Finally we set up the picnic on a blanket, set out plates, napkins and the food. My prize dish sat before us. Each of us took a piece of the golden brown chicken and bit into it.

No one told me that just because chicken is browned nicely on the outside does not mean it is cooked all the way through. One bite into the raw, bloody meat was enough for any of us. The chicken was tossed into the garbage. There was a lot of spitting and rinsing of mouths as I recall. That was my first and only date with John and his very cool convertible.

I had made no secret of my future plans with Danny, which perhaps contributed to my sparse date book. But occasionally a young man ignored the signs and pursued me regardless. That was flattering. It was not that I chose not to date, but to my mind any and all dates were temporary, a way of filling time until Danny was around and chose to pursue me. This I did not state openly, but it must have been conveyed because there was never a path to my door.

Bob was someone who chose to bypass it all. He was a senior to my junior status, a football star, scholar, headed to college, good looking, tall, muscular and fun to be around. We had several dates, and I realized he was getting serious. I explained to him as subtly as I could why the relationship was not going any farther. Ignoring what I thought was clear information, Bob said he loved me and would I marry him. It was my first marriage proposal and I did not take it seriously, but I was flattered. I explained to Bob that I could not marry him. Not to be deterred, Bob once more in a letter declared his love for me and repeated his marriage proposal. I once again declined, and eventually Bob gave up. He left for college that summer. I have wondered what became of Bob, where life took him and as any female would, I have wondered what if.

Dave was my last semi-serious boyfriend. Dave was my age, tall, dark hair, handsome, well-built and with a smile any artist would pay to capture. He too played football. Dave tended to be somber and serious, which I found somewhat appealing. The first time we began dating I am not certain which one of us did the pursuing, but I ended up wearing his class ring. The wearing of the class ring was a much coveted feat. The rings were big and bulky and always too large for a girlfriend's finger, which was the point of wearing it. To remedy the situation, yarn was wound around the ring until it stayed on your finger. Angora in pastel colors was the preferred yarn of the time. I chose baby blue. When people saw the oversized ring with yarn twisted into knots on your finger, you were then deemed important.

After a brief period of time, Dave decided he wanted to break off the steady dating arrangement. He sent a friend. His best friend, Bill, drove out to my house to tell me the sad news.

"Dave wants to break it off with you, Chris." Bill almost whispered the words to me at my back door.

"Why?" I asked.

"I don't really know, but he wants his ring back." Again, he was quiet.

"Well, okay." I took the ring off and handed it to Bill. I had no idea why Dave wanted the ring back nor did I understand why he did not wish to date me anymore.

"Where is Dave? Why didn't he come out here?" That much I wanted to know.

This time Bill looked me straight in the eye, "He's in the car waiting for me."

For this I had no answer. I shrugged my shoulders and said good night to Bill.

Before he walked out the door he said, "I'm really sorry."

I cannot say that I was heartbroken. But I thought it silly. Word spread like wildfire in school the next day. Evidently Dave and I had been quite an item around school, and so this was high drama. Not too long after Dave apparently changed his mind and pursued me once again. I had moved on and told him that dating him again was not going to happen.

"Danny is getting out of the service and will be home this summer," I told Dave as my explanation when he asked why.

"What makes you think he'll have time for you?"

"Well, I'm going to be around and available," I said.

"You're wasting your time, Chris," he said.

I did not believe him. I never believed anyone who attempted to deter me from my plan. In my mind the end result was set in stone. It was just a matter of waiting.

Dave was always a consummate gentleman, except for the dumping me via a friend thing. He treated me like royalty, showed me affection, and being with him was something I remember fondly. We made an attractive couple, which was certainly of utmost importance.

There were the occasional one-time dates along the way that are better left forgotten. Almost all of my memories of dating have slipped into a quiet place of fondness. Some I recall with smiles, some with genuine warmth and a few, a very few, with a slap to my head saying, "What was I thinking?"

Looking back, I was naïve and completely unarmed for understanding how a male-female relationship should be or might become. All that had been displayed before me, and all I had ever seen, was a play book on how to ruin a relationship, the ways to disrespect another human being, and the best way to make the worst relationship choices. I had never seen a man treat a woman with tenderness and caring. I never understood that a loved woman is a treasure to be valued and cherished by a man. I did not know that I was worth wooing and winning. And so I settled for what I had seen all my life. You take what you can grab, manipulate to win, accept lies as truth, and expect to be won and then treated as worthless.

CHAPTER TWENTY TWO

Emmett Farm House

My decision to live with my father was not out of devotion to my father or even a lack of love for my mother. My reasons were selfish and self-centered; much like my father's when he left his family to follow his mistress. In reality, I had set my face to capture a prize: Danny. I figured that if Milly moved in with my father, it was a foregone conclusion that that was where Danny would go when he got out of the service. He might not live there, but I was smart enough to see the obsessive hold Milly had on her children and devious enough to know that proximity would count in my favor. And I most unfortunately, was stupid enough to make myself ever so available. Life is sometimes cruel when we are stubborn and unrelenting.

Home life was rigid and lonely. In my desperate need to be accepted, I chose to ingratiate myself to Milly. I was tolerated at best, scorned more often than not, and ignored the rest of the time; all under the watching eyes of my father. I am not certain whether he chose to ignore how I was treated or if it was his attempt to keep the peace by placating Milly in all things. Whatever the reason, I never felt that I belonged there as Joe's daughter. Although Teresa was Milly's child, she did not fare any better. As a young girl, Teresa spent a great deal of time curled up in a fetal ball, sucking her thumb, and holding onto her security blanket. The two lovers were so intent on appearing blissful and content, nothing else mattered. It took all their energy to make believe all was well, life was grand and certainly the misery and destruction they foisted on so many innocent lives was worth it.

After just one year in Mt. Clemens, my father and Milly announced they had purchased a farm house in a place called Emmett. The move had not been discussed with us or within our earshot. We just packed up and headed to this place in the middle of nowhere. By now, my sister, Shirley Ann, had joined our family at Dysfunctional Central.

The house was a two story saltbox built sometime around before time began. The upstairs was one giant room with two small closet like rooms off the center, neither of which had any doors. Curtains hung on wooden rods to give a quasi-privacy effect. I had one of the tiny rooms and Shirley Ann and Teresa shared the large center room. My father and Milly had gone off one weekend before the move and were married. They went alone and returned after one weekend. That was that. Now married, they shared the remaining tiny bedroom.

Downstairs was a living room where a monster oil furnace stood that heated the house. Heat went upstairs by way of one enormous grate in the ceiling over the oil stove. It was primitive but effective. The dining room was directly off the living room. It was a formal room with a large rectangular oak table that sat the five of us comfortably. The kitchen was roomy as well; narrow but long and hosted a smaller table for meals on a less formal basis.

The back door, which was the only door we used, entered into a roomy space where we kept boots, coats, and whatever else found its way there. Off this space was the one and only bathroom. The bathroom was small and out of date but adequate. The most memorable thing about this bathroom was constantly being warned not to linger in the shower and use up all the hot water. "Don't use all the hot water" became a mantra I heard in my sleep. I believe this spawned my marathon showers later in life.

The Barn

Outside was a small structure that my father liked to imagine was a barn. It was not. It was a 10x10 shingled building that stayed standing by the Grace of God. Nevertheless, my father and Milly bought calves, put them in the shingled building and called it a barn. There were a few chickens, geese that I loved to chase when I could get away with it, and a duck or two. I did not fancy myself a farmer and except when I was forced to do chores, I had nothing to do with the farming. Farming was one of the fantasies the two, my father and Milly, built as an ideal for their life as they sat around our brown Formica kitchen table on Frazho Road, while my mother worked.

We did not have a telephone. I do not believe it was because of any financial hardships as much as the two lovers, like Marlene Dietrich, "vanted to be alone." However, for the three other resident females, one in high school, this was a problem. There was only one vehicle and my father drove that to wherever it was he happened to be working. This meant any extra-curricular activities available to a teenage girl were out of the question. It was not just a matter of no telephone and no available vehicle, but apparently our needs simply did not matter. What my sister and I wanted was never considered. In fact, we learned not to venture into wants or interests. We knew better. As a result, any special consideration or favor for Shirley or Christine became a war between my father and Milly. If there was any hint of my sister and me being considered apart from Milly, my father paid the price. And by extension, so did we. The three of us, Shirley Ann, Teresa and me, shared a common circumstance; we were simply there and were very much on our own.

So the five people living in the antiquated house settled into an oppressive way of life. My father and Milly desperately pretended to be happy and serene but lived on top of a powder keg ready to ignite at a moment's notice. And often it did. Our days were one of two atmospheric conditions. If my father and Milly were getting along, they were talkative with a form of forced happiness. They snuggled on the couch and played the blissful couple role. Milly cooked dinners each night for the master as he arrived home. We ate at the formal dining table, where my father, playing the role of land baron, served us all from his place at the head of the table. The conversations never included the three of us as in, "How was your day? How was school? What would you like to do tonight?" The truth was, neither of them gave much thought to anyone or anything but themselves.

Even on good days, which were few, it was a contest. Would Joe pay too much attention to Christine or Shirley Ann and not enough to Milly? This delicate peace, shattered at any moment like glass in a storm, never lasted long. When it did, it was replaced by the other atmosphere that would surface. Milly would become angry over some perceived slight. Her manipulation skills were superior and never failed to accomplish her goal. My father would respond in anger. He and Milly would end up screaming and fighting for an extended period of time. After the screaming, slamming of doors and/or cupboards, Milly would go up to their tiny bedroom and stay there. Silence. Now personally, I liked that part, but my father, having destroyed every other part of his life, knew that this was as good as it was going to get. He would have to salvage something of the then present situation. He would be mournful for a time. I would occasionally try to talk to him, to get close to him, to cheer him up and show interest but to no avail. I believe he was by this time afraid to show my sister and me any love or affection lest Milly become enraged over being slighted in some way all over again. This den of silence would go on for anywhere from two days to a week, depending on how long my father could hold out. One thing was certain however, he never made it very long. Milly was a marathon pouter. I have to give her that. She could set records, and I am sure she did.

During the siege Milly never left the bedroom. Teresa was her little slave, like a minion in the time of war. She would bring her mother hot tea to sustain her, snacks to starve off hunger, and occasionally just stay there to comfort the poor wounded soul. Life was hard under *Milly's Law*.

These quiet times were ones I enjoyed. The ranting and raving stopped. Screaming ceased. There was blissful quiet if only for a brief respite. But the occasional peace did not last. My father, without fail, went up to the garrison, literally crawling over to the bed where his love reclined and asked for forgiveness. And it was benevolently given, but at a greater cost each time. If everything that had occurred over the past years had not stripped my father of any self-respect he may have managed to salvage, this most assuredly put an end to any remnants. I wanted to tell them both how selfish they were and all the hell they had created, but because at sixteen years old I still valued my life and limb, I kept silent.

Our lives in Emmett on Stapleton Road became the stuff of legends. One night my friend, Lynn, was visiting. She had ridden the bus home with me from school and was spending the night. Dinner time came and we all sat at the beautifully set dining room table, linen table cloth and napkins carefully placed. I, of course was prepared, having been schooled early in life in good table manners. Meatloaf was the main course. My father sliced the meat, placed one on each plate and passed the plates around the table. So far, so good. There was no casual table talk, just six people sitting like idiot robots ready to consume food. And then my father ruined it. He asked Milly if we had any ketchup. What ensued was a tirade too ludicrous to repeat and too virulent to forget. Milly was livid that he should dare to suggest her meatloaf be desecrated by ketchup. Teresa, Shirley Ann and I were used to this but my friend Lynn sat in stunned silence. The only upshot was that we enjoyed two or three days of silence. Milly in the garrison, Teresa the minion running back and forth, and Shirley Ann and I ignored and on our own. My father withdrew into his usual dismal silence. I think in some perverse way it is why I love ketchup with my meatloaf to this day.

As wars go, the Ketchup War was a mild one. The first Thanksgiving in our Emmett farm fairyland was epic in proportion, and one I am certain is still talked about in the annals of Emmett history.

Living directly across the road from us was a genuine farm family, the Morgans. Bob and Marilyn Morgan were gentle quiet souls who raised seven children on a working farm. The farm spanned several hundred acres, had more than one barn and more animals than I could or cared to count. The Morgans were about to experience a form of reality TV before its time.

The night of the Turkey War began much like other nights at 2270 Stapleton Road. The mood was sullen and tense, with no one making small talk. That was normal for our house. Dinner was Thanksgiving leftovers; normally still a treat one day past, and served in the kitchen rather than the formal dining room. Like any time bomb, the settings for explosion were present whenever my father and Milly were in the same room. She brooked no competition even from her own child, and my father was always wound up tight and ready to explode. The two of them sat and stared. The same five people were trapped in a swirling swamp of menace and resentment like bubbling gas waiting for a match. As always, from whence the spark came remained a mystery.

Screaming and shouting ensued. My father grabbed the roaster full of turkey, dressing and juices, heaved it up high and slam dunked it into the garbage. Even for him, this was new in its magnitude of rage. It was both impressive and terrifying. Milly's shrill voice rose to a new height, bringing possible ear drum damage. Teresa and Shirley Ann sat in stunned silence, still at the table.

It seemed a foregone conclusion that dinner was over before it began, given that the turkey and fixings now resided in the kitchen garbage can. The kitchen table got slammed against a wall, scattering food, dishes, silverware and condiments. Ketchup was noticeable by its absence. While I do not remember who slammed the table, I am certain it was my father. Such a move was typical for one of his rages.

Thus fueled, the two love birds went out the back door, screaming, arms flaying, and headed to the road. Once centered in the road, each gave full vent to anger, self-disgust, shame, regret and blame. Only later did we learn that the entire Morgan clan, all nine of them, had front row seats from the three stories of their majestic farm house.

Inside, the real victims went about doing what, by now, had become second nature, scurrying around in fear to quickly clean up the mess left behind by the carnage of these two totally self-absorbed people. Another night at dinner with the Wener/Pechaceks.

One added bonus was, as always, a few days of silence as each went to his or her respective corners for a respite in between the insanity that was now the norm.

CHAPTER TWENTY THREE

My junior year at Memphis High School passed much like the two previous years. During my freshman and sophomore years we had moved three times and that meant Memphis High School was my third high school in thirteen months. There had not been enough time to make friends or get close to anyone. I did not mind. In fact, I liked being the new person at a school. Being new meant no one expected anything of you right away. Teenagers were no different than toddlers when a new kid came into the picture. Everyone circled the playground, eyeing the stranger, watching for anything different and weighing whether or not this unfamiliar face should be allowed inside the play area. It suited me fine. I was accustomed to being alone. The insanity that had become the norm in my family was too surreal to explain to outsiders. I could not even explain it to myself.

I did make friends at Memphis High School but slowly and cautiously. We lived several miles out of the town of Memphis, and because there was no way to get back and forth other than the school bus, extra-curricular activities were sparse. I had the short time during the school day to make friends before the bus took me home again. Without a telephone to keep me connected to my school friends, once the school bus dropped me off, my day was done. Walking through the back door of the farm house and into a universe of solitude was never a conscious thought. It was something that became a survival technique. Better to be invisible than a quacking target on display. What we did or did not do or say was irrelevant to the mood of the house at any given time.

My small upstairs bedroom was in the front of the house. I had one window, and it faced the dirt road we lived on, which connected to the other dirt road that led the three miles out to the highway, which led to nowhere. We lived between Emmett and Memphis, both small farming communities in the Michigan thumb area. Emmett consisted of a post office, manned by one person, a railroad track that never seemed to see a train, a small grocery store, one bar, one local eatery and one very large, beautiful turn of the century Catholic Church. There was one priest for the Parrish, and I believe he came with the church. There was one gas station, and it was usually busy with men on tractors who congregated there to discuss the weather, hay fields, and cows, and all things related to the weather, hay fields, and cows.

At the opposite end of my universe was Memphis. In comparison, Memphis was a thriving metropolis. There were two local restaurants, a bank, and several bars, one which served food and so called itself a bar/restaurant making it different from the other bars. There was a hardware store, drug store with a soda fountain, a meat market and bakery, and a pool hall. The pool hall was a local hangout for teenagers because it served hamburgers, fries and hot dogs. Once, a new family came to town and being entrepreneurial, turned one of the old stately homes into a fine dining establishment. This did not last. People in the area were not accustomed to white linen table cloths and matching napkins.

One business that did put Memphis on the map was the Vlasic Pickle Factory. This was located just outside of the downtown area. To be specific, all of the businesses were in the downtown area because they all lined Main Street which was two blocks long. The pickle factory was just around the corner from Main Street, which made it still downtown. The pickle factory employed a good portion of the population in Memphis. If you did not work on the farm full time, then the next best thing was a steady job at Vlasic Pickle Factory. All of the employees of the pickle factory had to wear white mesh hair nets. I decided early that working at the pickle factory was not a career choice in my future.

Some of my new high school friends had part time jobs. I wanted to get a job as well. There were jobs offered to me, all of which I had to turn down because I would have no way of getting to and from a place of business. Not being able to work and having few outside activities made for a very isolated life when you are a young teenager. It was not as though I had presented a plan to my father, had asked permission or expressed a desire for any of these things only to be told no. There had been no discussion, no thinking over a possible opportunity or even a heated discussion followed by the "because I said so" answer. The no discussion rule had been a part of my life ever since I could remember and was not new following the divorce and flight with the mistress. My father accepted no opinions other than his own. Growing up with that axiom, I had shut off the part of my brain that made plans apart from what my father dictated. I did not seriously entertain any ideas of independence or of what it would be like to experience something new.

In this house there was no other; there was my father and Milly. Shirley Ann, Teresa and I were like three poltergeists, invisible and silent for the most part. We blended into the fabric of the house. If there was cruelty from the adults who controlled our movements, it was subtle, maneuvered, and manipulated behind smiles and sighs. Nothing we said or did was acknowledged unless by way of chastisement or orders given as to what needed to be done at the precise moment. Each day consisted of our world only as it existed within the greater world of the two adults who controlled us. Silence was most often the best method of existing in our war zone. So we tiptoed around the landmines with our best hope being when one went off, we were not standing on top of the thing. But you just never knew.

A bright spot did appear once in a while as it did one afternoon in late fall. I had just gotten off the school bus, and my friend

Ella Morgan called me from her front porch. Ella was one of the Morgans who had been witness to the great turkey war as I liked to refer to the incident. Ella, two years my senior had become a close friend. Of the few friends I had made, Ella was the one who actually knew what my home life was like, not only because I confided in her, but because she had that clear, open view. It was not uncommon for an argument to end up outside. The insane part was I was not embarrassed by the display of two adults screaming at each other in the open air or even the tirade of profanity. I was frightened by it and just chose to hide and ride out the storm.

I waved to acknowledge her call and crossed over the road and jumped up on her porch rather than go home. She grabbed me and dragged me to her bedroom and shut the door.

"Danny's here!" She whispered a scream in my ear.

My mouth dropped open, "What? Really? How do you know? When?" All my words tumbled out at once.

This was exactly what I had planned when I had moved with my father. Until recently, Danny had been in Okinawa, Japan. I knew he was due home on leave but was not sure of the date. Ella knew every detail there was to know about Danny and my innocent lust for him. She had even read all his letters with me. He and I had been writing letters back and forth for the entire two years of his time in the service.

Letters are wonderful things. On the printed page you can express things you might not have the courage to say otherwise or should never say. We had developed quite a saucy correspondence over the months. For his part, he had been writing in flowery terms of being eager to see me for some interesting reasons. That is until the last letter written just before he flew back to the states.

To be specific, I was dumped. He was back-peddling as fast as he could. His reasons were poetic and meant to convince me that it was all for my benefit. In truth, I was too young, too innocent and too virginal to be bothered with when there were so many nubile females out there for the picking. He was just twenty-one years old and home for a fast and furious thirty days. The world held too many very eager, very willing and very experienced women for Danny Pechacek to waste valuable time on a girl who had no

intention of falling into his bed. Of course he had not said all
those things; but, although I was now a country girl and young, I
was not stupid. On my part, I was not going to be one more in a
line of here today, gone tomorrow female notches on his belt. And
it was a belt which came off too easily and too often. But I was still
wholly ignorant of what lay ahead and believed that saving myself
for the man I was to marry would be rewarded with love and devotion and faithfulness.

The misery surrounding me taught me the folly of whoring
around. Hopping on that wagon was not a choice for me. That
kind of life brought pain and darkness. Living on the corner of
Hell and Misery with two tormented, now permanent, residents
of what they had created, gave me the resoluteness to stand my
ground. I did not want my life to go the same, sad empty way.

Ella was laughing. She was as excited as I was. Over the months
I had shared every thought with Ella and we had talked endlessly
about my hopes and plans for a future with Danny so she was in
this with me.

"I saw him. Someone drove him here and dropped him off,"
she said.

I could not speak. My heart was pounding.

"Don't let anyone know I told you," she suddenly cautioned
me. "It's supposed to be a surprise."

"Ok." We giggled and hugged.

I left Ella's room, went down the stairs, out her front door
and casually walked across the road. When I walked in the door I
said a cheery hello to Milly as I passed through the kitchen. I was
impressed with my ability to remain calm and casual.

Milly said, "Can you take these clothes up and put them in your
room?" There was nothing unusual in the request. The short to
the point sentence was the depth and breadth of all our conversations. There was nothing unusual in that.

"Sure," I said in my most innocent voice. Grabbing the arm full
of clean laundry, I walked up the narrow staircase.

My bedroom door was a long curtain hanging from a wooden
rod. I pushed the curtain back. Danny was lying full length on my

small bed, smiling. At 6' 2", slender, tanned, and muscular, he was my definition of handsome. Dark hair, a strong nose that fit his long face, perfect white teeth and full lips, he was simply gorgeous. He had a smile that made me weak-kneed. He was the older man of all my romantic dreams, and I was predictably impressed by everything he said or did.

Without saying a word, I sat down on the side of my small bed. His arms came slowly around me, drew me close and kissed me. His kiss was warm and slow. He was practiced and deliberate and in full command of what he knew to be his desirability. I was none of those things. The boys I had allowed to kiss me were as ignorant as I was of what a kiss could be. I did not need to be told this was the real thing. There was no sincerity or genuine caring in his movements then, but for me it was everything.

The next few days were magical. I reveled in the occasional attention of this man that I had sworn as a green twelve year old to love forever. He spent his time regaling us all with stories of Okinawa. He was funny and articulate and arrogant. Nothing thus far in life had ever challenged him or been denied him. He possessed whatever was within his reach with no fear of rejection. We did not spend time alone other than brief moments while the rest of the house was doing other things. Regardless of my devotion for him, Danny was twenty-one to my sixteen and I knew that. He finally returned with friends to the city for what I could only assume was more experienced fun. Other than a few chaste kisses and a brief episode of petting as we called it, there had been nothing akin to the passion he wanted and was looking for. His reckless lifestyle and lack of belief for all things I held as valuable were lost in my fantasy vision of what I wanted life to be.

I lived in a world where I believed that truth would win out. I believed that faithfulness would be rewarded. I believed that loyalty would speak for itself and be returned in kind. I had never seen any of these things be successful in the life I was currently living, but I had created a fantasy world for my future in which they would.

I had no mirror of goodness, loyalty, truth or faithfulness to reflect back to me what was just and right. I had no role models to follow. I did not grow up being told I was smart or funny or beautiful. I did not hear that I could be successful in life, that others would find me valuable or attractive and be drawn to me and want to be my friend or may even want to marry me someday. As far as I was concerned, it was all up to me and I believed that Danny would actually be settling for less than the best if he chose me. So I had better pony up and be the perfect girl. That meant taking anything that was handed to me with no complaint, even lies and betrayal.

The adults in my life were void of advice even if I were to ask it of them. I was walking blind, testing what I believed to be right and hoping it worked.

Unfortunately, that plan did not work out so well.

CHAPTER TWENTY FOUR

My father died at forty-three years old. Too young. I was just seventeen years old and a junior in high school. One day at the end of January 1965 I got off the bus to see our neighbor, Marilyn Morgan, waiting for me. That was unusual in itself. Marilyn was a soft-spoken, quiet woman who rarely left her house and was not someone you would find waiting at your doorstep. My father had suffered a heart attack while at work, she told me. He had been taken to Lapeer General Hospital, and Milly was there with him now. I thanked her and walked into the house to wait. Without a telephone there was nothing to do but sit and wait until Milly or someone came by with news. We sat and waited, Shirley Ann, Teresa and me.

Late into the evening Milly returned home. My father was stable. It had been a severe heart attack, and so he would be in the hospital a number of days. That was all anyone could tell us. Open heart surgery was as yet in the future.

My brother, Nick, now in the Marine Corps, was notified and sent home on emergency leave. Danny, an Army Paratrooper stationed in Fort Campbell, Kentucky, was given emergency leave as well. Milly was understandably at the hospital almost continuously.

Shirley Ann and I visited once during the two weeks prior to my father's death. A priest came to visit my father.

Although long gone from the Catholic Church or any religious affiliation, my father listed his faith as Catholicism. He and his siblings had been brought up in the Catholic Church, and he had never considered himself anything other than Catholic. During the visit, the priest informed my father that in order to receive any sacraments, he must first denounce Milly as his wife. The church did not recognize divorce and certainly that adultery thing was frowned upon. While I was not opposed to the denouncing requirement, it made me angry that this priest would deny my father a sacrament that would have brought him a sense of peace. Still young and hopeful, I held to the notion that the priest was the only and almighty voice of God. After that, I decided maybe this was not the God I wanted to believe in.

Several days passed and it appeared that my father was recovering. In the hospital and confined to bed, he seemed to be making progress toward a full recovery. Nick and Danny both returned to their respective bases. It seemed the worst was over, and now it was just a matter of regaining his strength and learning to live post-heart attack.

My father died suddenly on February 2, 1965. Late in the evening while alone in his hospital room, he mentioned to a nurse that he was feeling pain in his leg. She left the room to get medication, and when she returned he was gone. Medicine being what it was in 1965, an undetected blood clot had dislodged from a spot in his leg, traveled to his heart and he died.

It was late into the night when Milly was summoned to the hospital, and later still when she returned home to tell us that my father was gone. That was it. Shirley Ann was sobbing. Teresa, crying, embraced her mother. Milly, crying with deep soulful hurt, held Teresa, and the two of them walked away to in some measure share their grief. For her part Teresa was doing what she always did, comforting and sustaining Milly. It was a role she was practiced in, but not equipped at thirteen years old to perform. Shirley Ann and I stood alone. My sister went upstairs to the large bedroom she shared with Teresa to cry alone. I turned and went into the living room, sat in a soft cushioned wing-back chair, and curled my body up tightly as possible. I put my hands over my face and cried into the chair where no one could see my face or hear my sobs. The sense of aloneness overwhelmed me.

For the remainder of the night, we stayed isolated, as was our norm. Milly, comforted by Teresa in her small room. Shirley Ann, alone on her bed. Me, alone in the dark on a chair. I could not console my little sister. I did not give her my arms as comfort. Neither did I receive the comfort of arms around me. There was no one to share my grief. I no longer had even the semblance of being connected to a living soul, someone I belonged to within the walls of this pseudo-home. Just as our lives had been twenty-four hours previously and for months, we were people living under the same roof, each separate, not touching physically or emotionally.

I was truly alone now. I ceased to be Joe's daughter, the only protection left to me, and now that was gone. My mother was still living in the house where we all grew up, but that night she seemed even farther away than before. We did not hear from her and still had no means of communication by which to reach her on our own. No one asked us if we wanted to call her or somehow reach her. Waves of panic flooded over me, but there was no place to go, no place of refuge where I might flee until this awful wave of grief passed. It seemed no one cared. I think perhaps my tears were as much for myself as for my father. The thought crossed my mind that I was now at the mercy of a woman who had, at best, tolerated my presence and saw me as an unfortunate result of a war she had fought and won.

I wanted to be held in the arms of someone who cared about my grief. I wanted hands to stroke my face, wipe my tears, and say soft compassionate words of comfort to me. I wanted there to be someone to reassure me that my world would go on and that I would be safe. But as it had been in the past, there was no one.

Nicky came home on leave once again. Danny too arrived home. Janet, Milly's daughter and her husband, came immediately. Milly was surrounded by her children who held her and comforted her. They drew into a private circle of grief and sorrow; all of them united in their determination to protect their mother, help her and meet her needs as the grief swept over her. Shirley Ann and I stood alone as they all grieved. We stood alone not just metaphorically but physically. Milly and her comforters went upstairs with her to comfort her. No one spoke to either of us. We were excluded in this as in all other things concerning Milly and her children.

He had been our father, our connection to life, but this grief displayed was not for Joe and his death, it was for Milly's loss. We did not come under the wings of comfort and sympathy. No one really noticed our presence. My father's death was not the real tragedy; it was a precursor that caused pain to Milly. And as in all things, her family reacted to Milly's needs, her cries for help to the exclusion of all else. Shirley Ann and I were the interlopers, moving unbidden into their world. They had not asked for this intrusion any more than we had asked for theirs in our world. We, all seven children, became chess pieces moved on a board in a game we did not ask to play.

Friends from school came to the funeral home to pay their respects. Parents of friends came. They were strangers to me and could not fathom my grief, my sense of loss and the panic that the only world I knew was now gone. Strangers would not understand how truly alone I was, we both were, Shirley Ann and me. How could they? Theirs was a world with connections, with mother and father, siblings, all woven together by the threads of a shared history. Theirs was a foundation of caring and responsibility. That was not, nor had ever been a part of my life.

Relatives came. My aunts and uncles came to pay their respects to their brother's widow. In his life, my aunts and uncles had not approved of my father's abandonment of his wife and family but loved him with the complete love that only siblings can give. In his death, they gave proper respect and sympathy to his widow. For us, his children, there was little. We stood alone, on the outskirts of what was happening. No one inquired as to our future. No one offered aid should we need it. No one gave a thought as to our future with this widow, who, in their estimation, had been a partner along with their brother in the destruction of his family.

My father had been close with his siblings, but the familial ties had been broken following the divorce, in part because his siblings did not approve of what he had done, and also because their disapproval was not easily born by Milly. Now it appeared easier to stay aloof. Shirley Ann and I stood in a limbo, not belonging to my father's family but neither could we penetrate the circle of Milly's world.

The funeral passed quickly and quietly. Although the priest who had visited my father at the hospital before he died agreed to officiate at his funeral, he protested at burying his body in a Catholic Cemetery, avowing that the ground was more holy than regular ground. My father's refusal to denounce his current wife made it a problem as far as the church was concerned. As far as I was concerned, it was cold, hard dirt and did not represent anything more than a place to hold the empty shell that had once been my father. Someone prevailed, because my father's body was buried in the Catholic Cemetery. I was not sure if that desecrated holy ground or if my father was blessed to be there, six feet under, dead.

Life went on. I went back to school. Shirley Ann and Teresa went back to school. Winter ended and spring came. The sun came out, the wind blew, it rained occasionally, and it became summer. Nothing changed.

Milly, Teresa, Shirley Ann and I began spending occasional weekend visits with Janet at her home in Berkley. There was nothing to hold Milly to Emmett any longer. And sitting idly on weekends in awkward silence was something we all wanted to avoid, even if no one said it out loud. The farm house and the dream of becoming farmers had been shared by my father and Milly as a way to cloister them in a world they alone created and lived apart from prying eyes and reflections of the carnage they created. With her partner in this made-up existence gone, Milly moved on. She sold the house, and we moved into a rented house in Memphis. We all attended school in Memphis so it seemed a practical thing to do.

The house was a spacious two-story on a paved highway and close to town. It had a large bedroom upstairs, a kitchen, with a bathroom off the kitchen, a large living room with two spacious bedrooms, one on either side of the living room. The move did not feel so much like a new beginning for all of us as much as it felt like shutting a door on all memories of my father's existence. I slipped in easily, leaving behind life as a daughter and became an adult, on my own. Teresa, Shirley Ann and I, continued to live solitary lives. Stepping around real emotions, positive or negative, was too deeply engrained now and would not change for any of us.

One significant event did come about that altered my life forever. Danny's tour of duty in the Army ended. He was discharged in early May of 1965. We had continued our correspondence, and the letters carried the same musings and hints at a future together. For my part, I had not changed my mind regarding my feelings for him but his for me remained clouded, kept vague and out of sight in case he needed a quick escape. I was still young, naïve and inexperienced. The normal questions of a young girl in love for the first time swirled in my head. What was I supposed to do? How do I act or react? What was wise and what was foolish in this situation? He was an older man in my eyes. I had no confidante, no female to give me sage advice. I was again swimming in dark waters alone, dodging that Creature from the Black Lagoon.

Being alone and believing myself to be very adult, I followed the only course of action I thought was right. I considered myself in love with Danny and was already committed to him in mind and body. That had come when I was just twelve years old, and nothing over the past five years had changed my mind. So I did the only thing that seemed reasonable to me, I told him so. I was too naïve and too blatantly honest to understand that games were a requirement in life and certainly so with this man who saw all females as his for the taking and discarding. I had no games to play. Every answer to him was real, my feelings were open and sometimes raw, my devotion complete, and my faithfulness to him sealed. Naïveté assumed that my openness and honesty would be returned in kind. It was not. Instead it was mocked by his continued need for females to conquer and then abandon. He was his mother's son, but at seventeen years old I could not see the hurt that was before me. Again, as before, I was convinced that my complete devotion would be something appreciated and respected.

Following my father's death, Milly sought solace with an older gentleman from Memphis, a successful, semi-wealthy married farmer. He took her places and bought her expensive gifts. During the visits to Janet's house, Milly met a somewhat younger man. They began an affair He was married at the time. I neither judged nor opined in any way regarding what went on. Milly was a widow. I was dependent upon this woman for my existence, and so not only did I keep silent, as I had learned to do all my life, but neither did I allow my brain to engage in thoughts of right or wrong. That would be futile. Her penchant for married men did, however, affect my behavior.

I became obsessive with being honest, faithful and committed to one man, Danny. In my mind I would become the model of what a woman should be. He would see all my virtue and appreciate me as a rare gem. That was not exactly what happened.

CHAPTER TWENTY FIVE

My senior year of high school was decidedly different than the three previous years. I had made some good friends and had begun to feel comfortable being involved in school activities. After my father's death I was truly on my own even though I still lived in the house with Milly. Other than checking in as to my whereabouts, no one cared where I was or what I was doing. One major improvement was that I now ate hot lunch with my friends.

Memphis High School was built in 1895 and other than bathrooms now being indoors, it had not changed much since the doors first opened. It was a three story brick building. The main doors were heavy, thick solid oak. The polished wooden stairways were wide oaken steps with ornate handrails. All the classroom doors stood seven feet tall, solid oak, with small frosted panes of glass at the top. The wooden floors creaked with every step and not one was level. We had classrooms, a study hall, main office, janitor's room, shop class, home economics room and bathrooms. What this magnificent historic school building did not have was a place to cook or eat lunches. Because the high school was located one block from Main Street, it made it convenient to walk up town and eat at one of the local restaurants or the pool hall. One other option for lunch was to eat a school cafeteria hot lunch served at the elementary school, which was referred to as the new building. It had been built sometime after 1940. It was located two miles from the high school. And that was a problem.

Anyone from the high school intending to eat hot lunch on a particular day would go to the main office and buy a lunch ticket for that day. It was also possible to purchase five tickets at once and so be prepared for the whole week. At noon, ticket in hand, you hopped on a waiting school bus that took you to the elementary school cafeteria. From there you went through the line, surrendered your ticket and received a tray with the hot food choices of the day. Once finished, you returned by bus to the high school. The whole process was, by anyone's standard, painfully simple.

For me, it was immobilizing. One of the rules in our family was never make an independent decision, especially if you are a child. Although this was an implicit rule, I knew it was fixed and never up for discussion. If you veered from the rule, the consequences were swift and usually painful. Once as a young girl, I had stood before my father asking to go to a friend's house. My father said an immediate no. I opened my mouth and said, "But. . ." It was the only word out of my mouth before my cheek felt the hard slap. No one questioned my father. There was never any debate or discussion. No independent thinking.

Living with my father and Milly, I had lived with silence and learned to be comfortable in solitude. I understood that I had no one to depend upon but myself. At the same time, I lived in fear of stepping into any unknown territory. I avoided any situation where I did not know, and could not predict, the outcome and every step leading to a conclusion. For me, to err in doing something, or fail in an attempt at something new most assuredly would bring displeasure. And displeasure brought attention, and it was never positive attention. So being silent, immobile, and as much as possible, invisible was always safer. Detaching myself from situations I could not control helped me survive. The whole hot lunch thing was full of unknowns as far as I was concerned.

After one particularly nasty day walking up town to eat, I decided to go for hot lunch. For several days I carefully observed the process so I could memorize the moves and follow flawlessly along. Then I bought my ticket. I was committed. The day and the lunch passed without incident. No one screamed at me that I had done something wrong or had broken a rule that I was not aware was in place. The hot lunch was delicious. From that bold move, I was ready to branch out.

I decided to try out for cheerleading. The uniforms were cute and everyone admired a cheerleader, especially on game day when you got to wear the outfit to school. The try-outs were held after school in the elementary gymnasium because in 1895 they did not have the foresight to include a gymnasium in the building plan. To try out each girl had to do a prescribed cheer, a cartwheel and a jump or two. One by one each participant went out on the floor in front of the judges and did a cheer. It was my turn. I strode confidently to the front, faced the judges, and gave my name. I was given the go-ahead to begin. The bleachers were full of bored high school students, including most of the senior males from our class.

I began. Hands on hips, start the shout, wave arms in the air, do the jump and end with a cartwheel. Every move went perfectly. I was feeling confident and heady with upcoming success. Hands went over my head; I let my body go to the side into the cartwheel. I concentrated on keeping my legs stiff and straight as I went over. My hands touched the floor, arms straight and rigid, holding my body high in the air. And then, disaster. My wrist gave out, my arm crumpled, and I hit full force onto the floor. Lying in a rumpled heap in front of the judges, friends and attractive males was not part of my plan. I picked myself up and walked away with as much dignity as was possible; given just seconds ago I was a rolling mass of arms and legs. I did not make the cheerleading squad.

My next attempt at a team sport was basketball. I was suited to play basketball, even if I did not fully realize it at the time. Tall, lithe, strong arms and legs, and quick, making the team was easy. Practices were fun. I enjoyed running and learning the skills involved. The first game arrived, a home game. The stands were crowded. Basketball at Memphis High School was a popular sport. Students and parents turned out in full force for the games.

Game time. Our coach put me in to play from the start. We ran up and down the court, passing the ball, shooting baskets, scoring, and occasionally stealing the ball from the opposing team. The game had morphed into excitement. I was doing well, not spectacular, but gaining confidence as the game went on. It was a new feeling for me, being part of a team, being included in this camaraderie. Then it happened. I made an independent decision. I took charge of a situation. I went into new territory.

In one instant I went from guarding the girl next to me to managing to steal the ball. This was what victory was all about. In a flash I was dribbling the ball down the court towards the basket. The crowd roared. My teammates were screaming. Even my coach was up on her feet shouting to me. Their cheers made me run faster, dribble furiously, and my shot into the basket was perfect. I smiled to my team. Only then did I realize my magnificent shot had been into the other teams' basket. The two points went to our opponents. The shouts and calls had not been for my wondrous skills, but an attempt to stop me. And that was the end of my basketball career. Once more it was solidified in me, do not make independent decisions. Do not venture forth into new territory.

My final attempt at something new and adventurous was track. Track seemed harmless enough. Run around the track. Sometimes jump hurdles. And because track events were not well attended, it was a good time of just hanging out with friends. Track involved more sitting and waiting for the next event than any actual events. It seemed that I was best suited to the high jump. That was according to my coach, who was also the basketball coach. The high jump was a slow, not very competitive event, and I did have those long legs going for me. If there was a second string for the high jump, I was it. Another girl on the team was the expert high jumper and she excelled at it. I was there because, like some work of art you like but cannot quite fit into the décor, the coach found someplace to put me. My career in track was unremarkable.

More memorable than any sport I attempted was the near scandal I became a part of during my senior year. Having nailed down the ride-the-bus-eating thing, I was almost daily on the noon bus to and from the cafeteria. Memphis High School had acquired new teachers in the fall, two young men awaiting entrance to medical school. They both needed the income and since they were qualified as teachers, they applied for, and obtained teaching positions. As an added duty, they also offered to drive the lunch buses. These two men were attractive and young, both fresh out of college. Ben took notice of me, a close notice. We spent time in conversation, which I now realize was certainly a way of flirting. I was just seventeen years old at the time but looked older. I was very flattered by the attention.

In the fall, our senior class had put on a fall festival get together at someone's farm house. Both of the visiting teachers came along and partied with us. Ben and I had evidently caught the attention of some adult as we sat and talked for a long time. The evening ended. I was driving back with some girlfriends, and as I said good night Ben leaned over and kissed me. Not a peck on the cheek, a lip kiss. I was surprised but not displeased.

The next day in school, the senior class counselor called me into her office. Mrs. Martel was skinny, wore large rimmed glasses, dressed a little wild for small town Memphis and wore her long red hair coiled on top of her head. I loved her. She was a little crazy and out there someplace I envied her being able to go.

"Christine, do you know why I called you in to see me?"

"No. Am I in some sort of trouble?" This was always my first assumption when singled out for attention.

"Well not exactly," she was smiling. "But I do need to talk to you about something that evidently happened last night." The smile never left her face.

"I really don't know what you're talking about. I was with everybody else at the party. We all left by around 10 o'clock." I had no idea what was coming next.

"Well our principal has asked me to speak to you about some behavior he feels was inappropriate," she was nodding as she spoke.

I was shaking my head, still wondering what awful thing I had done that would come to the attention of the principal of the high school. Inappropriate behavior in any form was something

I avoided the same way I kept away from the Creature from the Black Lagoon.

"Well, apparently," she paused and grinned, "You were seen kissing Ben at the party."

Relief flooded over me and I shook my head. Then I laughed. We both laughed. I had been seeing Mrs. Martel for several weeks now and I was comfortable being open with her.

"Yes, we did," now I was smiling. "It was very nice too. He is very attractive."

"Honey, I don't see a thing wrong with it. You two are practically the same age, well almost. He's damn handsome and successful! And, he obviously finds you attractive. I say good for you." She slapped my knee as she said it.

"I know. Can you believe that?"

"Oh hell yes I can believe it. You are one pretty gal. But, and here's the thing," she leaned in closer to me, "you need to keep it out of sight as long as you are a student and he is a teacher. Okay?"

"I understand that. I don't think it's anyone's business but I see your point. But" I said, "and here's the thing, I really am in love with Danny." She knew that whole story. "I do think Ben is very handsome and nice but. . .," my voice trailed off.

"Got it," she said. "Actually I think what's really going on here is that the principal is jealous!" We both laughed at that. "It's hard for some of the males around here to remember that you are still in high school." She winked at me.

Handsome Ben did get into medical school shortly after that and we never saw each other again, which was a pity.

I managed to find employment that same year. There was a local woman who did catering for various area events, primarily wedding receptions. Being a Catholic community, all weddings were on Saturday before noon with the reception later into the evening. Gert, the caterer, hired high school kids to work the reception. We were young, strong, liked to stay up late, eat the extra food, and we worked for $5 an event and happy to get that. For our $5 in cash we unloaded the catering van, set up tables, helped with cooking, served either a sit down meal or kept the buffet going, served coffee, tea, pop and water and then did the clean up afterwards, washing dishes by hand. We cleaned all the tables, pots and pans, and utensils, put it all away, swept the floors, and loaded things back into the van. We earned our cash for sometimes up to ten hours on your feet and running. That's 50 cents an hour. And we lined up to do it. For me, it was money I earned, money of my own to spend and most importantly, it was getting out and being with people doing something independently.

If living with my father and his new wife had been solitary and lonely, living with just Milly was intensely so. As long as my father was alive, I had some connection to the world they had created. I was a daughter, undeniably connected to the universe in which they lived. Being connected did not afford any privileges as far as attention, affection or approval, but I belonged somewhere and for a reason.

After my father's death, that flimsy thread of connection evaporated. Suddenly I was no one. My identity, however tenuous, was swallowed up and digested into the vacuum that once was my father.

CHAPTER TWENTY SIX

My senior year was opening up for me. It was the beginning of serious trouble in Viet Nam as well. The young men who were my friends were well aware of the growing conflict, and so the draft was uppermost in their minds. But many of my friends were talking of college plans. Despite top grades and a talent for learning, I had never considered attending college. For one thing, it was never discussed in my family. We were of that class of people for which advanced learning seemed out of reach and unnecessary for the limited opportunities we accepted in life.

Another factor, more real although not identifiable except in retrospect, were the actions and attitudes of the adults who controlled our lives as we grew. Our futures were not discussed as being separate from any impact we may or may not have on their own lives. My father and mother did not speak of a career for me as an adult, of my being a success as I grew, or possibly achieving a life above the one they now lived. I am convinced this was because they could not see beyond the immediate misery of their own lives. Struggling to get through one day at a time affords little room for dreaming of a better future for themselves or their offspring.

Despite my parents' lack of vision for my life, the overriding reason for not seeing college in my future was, of course, Danny.

I convinced myself that to be out of sight was to be out of mind. This proved to be true, but in a more tragic way as our lives became entwined.

I am not certain that what occupied my mind could be called plans as much as it was a blind obsession. It was the same thing that had been in my head since I was twelve years old. Danny was once again a civilian, home from his three years of active service. That meant he would be seeing his mother, my once step-mother. I say once, because following the death of my father some six months previously, I was unclear as to what that made our relationship, mine and Milly's. In truth, we had no relationship, merely a connection, but even that vanished with my father's death. I believe that we, my sister and I, were allowed to stay in the household because there were monetary rewards in the way of Social Security death benefits. It was practical. Milly had no means of employment and no skills that would have been marketable. The money was necessary for her to live. Teresa's father continued to pay child support but that was not a large sum of money and did not go far. I understood practical. And I had no illusions that my sister and I were anything else.

The arrangement served my ends as well. Danny was out of the service, and I wanted to be around Danny. Living with Milly made that doable. It was foolish, but again I had no role model for wise and prudent. I was on my own. I was playing at being an adult and what was particularly tragic, was that I believed it would all come together for a Cinderella life.

Danny and I began dating that summer. At first it was just being with family, his family. There were gatherings at the beach, an occasional BBQ, or a family dinner. They were not dates as in he asked me to go somewhere with him and I agreed. In fact, I simply appeared whenever he was around. So there was no asking. I was not pursued and chosen. My appearance was more like a dandelion you simply cannot get rid of, pretty, but still a nuisance and not a thing of beauty to be cultivated, chosen and cared for. Having long ago forgotten who I was as a person or even that a separate me existed, I just kept popping up, trying to imitate the type of woman I thought Danny wanted.

Poor Dan. He deserved better. We both did. He had no opportunity to even know me, the person I was or the woman I might become. I did not even know that about myself. We gradually grew into dating on a more real basis. Our first date, as in would you like to go somewhere with me, was to a drive-in movie theater. Needless to say, I was ecstatic. This was it. Showtime!

Danny had purchased a car once he had settled back in Michigan. Before he went into the service, he had that dream car, a 1957 Chevrolet Convertible, black with a white top, and red leather interior. I had looked forward to riding in that car one day, sitting close to Danny as he drove, but it never happened. While he was in the service, Milly sold the car for some ready cash. She pocketed $700 quick money, and the sexiest car on the road was no more. His current vehicle was a 1961 Pontiac Bonneville, blue on blue with blue leather interior. It was very nice but still, I felt cheated on time in the '57 Chevy. It was a tragedy. I would have looked stunning sitting in that car. And riding together, Danny and I could only have been described as spectacular.

Once parked at the drive-in theater, the speakers hooked to the windows, we settled in to watch two films, a cartoon or two, and the little hot dog people, talking popcorn, and dancing drinks parade across the screen. Danny soon fell sound asleep. I suspected that he was not as ecstatic to be out on a date with me as I with him. Perhaps my charm and wit were not as scintillating as I had imagined. This date was not turning out as I had dreamed it would. Still, we were on a date. Sometime into the second movie, Danny woke up.

"I fell asleep. I'm so tired from working all day," he said. "I'm sorry."

I laughed. "That's fine."

In truth, it was anything but fine. I was disappointed and hurt. The glow of being on a date with him became a bit tarnished. After the movie, we went to a local restaurant for something to eat. I ordered a tuna sandwich. I did not even like tuna fish but was intimidated by Danny's casual, slightly arrogant attitude, so I wanted to order something small and cheap. How that smooth move was going to impress him, I had no idea, but once again, I aimed to please.

After the restaurant he drove to a secluded spot and parked. He drew me close and began kissing me. He was slow and gentle, patient and certainly mindful of his attraction. I was totally out of my depth, a little frightened but eager to learn and paralyzed with the thought that he might find me too innocent for his bother. However, how eager never became fully realized because a flash-light suddenly appeared through Danny's window.

"Good evening, Sir. Can I ask what you are doing parked here?" The police officer was polite but not smiling.

"We're just talking, Officer." Danny's reply was equally polite but not friendly. The flashlight was then directed to my face.

"Good evening, Miss. Everything okay here?" He let the light move from my face downward.

Damn, I thought, how did those buttons on my blouse get undone?

"Yes," I answered.

The light made a quick survey of the car, front and back, land-ing finally on Danny's face.

"Sir, I think you and the young lady need to move on." His voice was quiet but firm and demanding.

"Officer, we're getting married, and we haven't seen each other in a while." Danny's voice matched the officer's. I wondered how many times that line had come from his lips and with how many females. Suddenly the romantic feelings I had been experiencing evaporated.

"Well, Sir, I suggest you move on before you have to." With that he walked away.

I remember hearing "smart ass" or something similar from Danny. We left. The incident made me realize how out of my shal-low depth I was. At this point I began asking myself some serious questions. Was I ready for a sexual relationship with this man? And certainly he was a man, not one of the teenage boys I had known to this point. But since it was always easier to put off seri-ous thinking, I dismissed any trepidation I had. Unfortunately, I also ignored the fact that Danny's goal was different from mine.

Mine was, as always, a life together with this man, my whole life. I was ill-equipped to comprehend what his goal was, if indeed he had one at all, other than the obvious.

Later in the summer we were on a date to the Armada Fair. This fair was typical of small town county fairs everywhere. It was early evening, and we walked the midway. I was so enthralled merely being with this man, I grinned incessantly. A couple of weeks before we had for the first time, begun a sexual relationship. My first. My only. It was frightening in a new way for me. I was both excited at the new feelings Danny's lovemaking evoked in me and giddy with the sense of belonging. As immature as it was, this was like arriving where I belonged, had always belonged. I was spinning into an abyss I did not know existed. It never occurred to me that there would ever be any man in my life but this man, that I would ever give myself to anyone but to Danny. Even now it is difficult for me to comprehend the foolishness of that decision. I did not think it through. I did not count the cost both to my soul and to my heart. From that first time I was sealed to this man, there was no turning back; my fate was set. I had never been so dangerously vulnerable and alone. In my mind, stepping into a world of physical intimacy was final and irrevocable. I was now a part of him, linked by more than a first time sexual encounter. The consequences of my decision were to be played out over the next five decades and bring heartache and pain I could not imagine existed.

At the fair we walked to the Ferris wheel. Danny bought our tickets and up we went. The midway had never looked more thrilling than from the slow, high ride of the Ferris wheel. We sat close together in the car, his arm around me, pulling me close. The music floated up to us as the wheel ground around and around.

"This time next year we'll be husband and wife," Danny said as he stared, unflinchingly into my face.

Did I hear that right? My heart was pounding loud enough that I could hear its thud-thud over the music. I just smiled. I was speechless. I'm sure I looked like one of those stupid prizes at the games on the Midway; the Cupie doll with the frozen grin.

The ride ended, and we stayed at the Fair until late into the night. Still, I remained silent. I made no comment.

Not another word was mentioned about his declaration on the Ferris wheel. We did not talk of plans for the future. Nothing was said of when, where or how. Although I remained seemingly dumb and incapable of speaking to Danny about anything as real as my deepest feelings and emotions, I did immediately and foolishly tell Milly, his mother, who then went to Danny.

"Did you propose to Chris?" she asked.

"Well, I brought the subject up. But nothing is final. I am thinking about it." He stumbled over himself backtracking.

The sucking sound of words being taken back and swallowed echoed in the room. For my part, I treated a private and sacred moment with little respect. Instead of affording this man the respect due his right as a man in one of the most important decisions of his life, I ran fast and furious like a jackal after the kill. Rather than waiting and allowing him his right to authority, I superseded that authority, and not for the last time in our lives.

So instead of the memory of a sweet proposal, a romantic encounter, it became a matter of being cornered into a decision. As I look back, I believe Danny felt more obligated, even a little trapped into something that was in reality an idea, a testing of the waters and not a life decision. For all I knew, it may have been another line he used to secure a continuing sexual relationship. Perhaps at this point, love had not yet replaced physical passion for him. But that was to come silently to his heart and as deeply as my own.

We talked later and in private.

"I do intend to marry you, but I was just thinking out loud back then." He smiled.

Panic. Again, as would become my behavior for the next four decades, I said nothing. I did not respond with a question or demand what he meant. I sat back and prayed he would want me, as always thinking myself unworthy.

Danny had been out of the service and in civilian life just three months. Neither he, nor, I were ready for a life decision. Neither of us knew anything about life. We both just played at what we had learned and saw from the adults around us. For me that meant running far and wide of the suicidal decisions and tragic consequences I had watched adults make again and again. At least I thought I was running away from the mistakes. In truth, I was merely fashioning then into my own version of insanity. Danny had been witness to his own version of hell played out in his life and home.

His ignorance to the world that existed within my life was evidenced when, coming home on leave, he first learned his parents had divorced. Nothing had been said. No one had told him anything. Neither his father nor his mother treated him as a cherished son, a loved child taking care to sit down and explain what was happening. His life was forever altered but it was of no consequence in the balance of selfishness for conquest of the only thing that mattered to either of those adults, their own needs.

He might have been an adult outwardly, standing tall, speaking with bravado, but his little boy heart had been crushed by the two people sworn to love him and put his life before their own. He spiraled out of control, doing what he had always done, finding approval in all the wrong places and in the only way he had been trained. Danny had no role model to walk him through what it was to be a man, a loyal husband, friend and lover. Just as it had been since he was a young boy, he was on his own. Sink or swim. Live or die. And survive at all costs.

As for me, I was just as much on my own as he. And that was how our engagement began.

CHAPTER TWENTY SEVEN

I believe the official engagement began sometime in the early fall of 1965. But truth be told, it is unclear. There had been the questionable proposal on the Ferris wheel at the Armada Fair and my foolish declaration to Milly. Following that, our lives became routine. My senior year in Memphis was in full swing. Perhaps swing is too strong a word for what could best be described as a slow wave. My friends were enjoying all the last days of high school, senior skip days, senior trip, football games, rallies, and being carefree and a little crazy.

I, on the other hand, was focused on marrying Danny. I consciously let every opportunity to enjoy being a teenager and to make life long memories slip by. My days were spent behaving above reproach in all areas of my life. Aware that Milly was watching me, I allowed no opportunity for even a hint that she might disapprove of me or my actions and inform Danny. Milly held steel control on all of us, whether living in the house or not. Danny lived and worked in Royal Oak but was tied to her control as surely as if a bungee cord remained knotted securely around his waist. At any given time a spoken word or command would be the pull snapping him back. Outwardly she appeared the understanding benevolent mother smiling on her children, watching as they grew in life; but inwardly, the cords remained strong. Should it become necessary, Milly pulled tight and any one of her children, or all three, rushed to her side ready for whatever may be required for her comfort or advancement.

I knew that any day or at any moment, I could easily be one of the damned should I fail to walk the imaginary line she held with absolute authority. Walking the tightrope of her approval was non-negotiable. One word, one hint from her to Danny that I was in some way not acceptable and it was over. Danny would believe his mother. If, on the outside chance, he reasoned that her disapproval was not warranted, it would not matter. No one defied or displeased her and certainly not Danny, the only son. From early in his youth, he had been trained to be her protector and defender. Right or wrong did not enter the picture. And so for me, it would be over. Period.

In some aspects, Danny was still the small boy terrified that his mother would leave him alone and frightened if he did not obey her unquestionably. Her influence was a fortress that could not be breached. You did not have an original idea, an opinion of your own, and to stand in defiance was unthinkable. Unlike my father before her who ruled by fear, Milly was quiet and subtle in her control. Her tools were secrets, whispers, and when needed, lies. I was terrified of Milly. Not because she shouted, raised her voice or ever raised her hand to me, but my life was dependent on her yea or nay. She had the power to snub out the tenuous foundation under me. Her virulent need for control of her son's life would not happen then, but a few short years into the future her venom would seep into our lives causing a breach that almost destroyed what we did have. Almost.

But back then, I remained safely tucked away in a cocoon, coming out on the weekends when Danny drove to Memphis. My week consisted of high school for three hours, as I only needed three credits to graduate, and then four hours of employment. Living close to town meant that I could find a job. I worked in Becker's Meat Market and Bakery for $1.25 an hour. Like the catering I had done earlier, the work was hard but interesting. I spent every minute of those hours on my feet hustling. It was an informative job as well, giving me lifelong useful information. I learned to cut up a whole chicken with lightning speed. And I learned which cuts of beef were tender and which would be tough. Some people go through their whole lives not having such information. At the end of each week, I sent my entire paycheck to Danny who put it in a joint savings account we had opened. This money would go to a down payment on a house we intended to purchase prior to the wedding.

While my friends were doing what most teenagers did and making memories along the way, I was being safe and quiet at home, waiting for the weekends. Danny was working a sheet metal apprenticeship, sharing an apartment with his father and continuing to date any woman he wished. He lived two lives with impunity, pretending to be the faithful engaged lover on the weekend and then dating and having as much sex with other females as he could track down. Something was wrong with this picture, but like someone in a 3-D movie theater without benefit of 3-D glasses, I stumbled along in my safe darkness.

Our Lady of Mt. Carmel, Emmett

Definite plans for the wedding began to take shape. We choose June 25, 1966 as the wedding date. It was, of course, a Saturday morning. I never understood the reasons behind the day and time mandates of the Catholic Church. The church was chosen, and even that was a decision not made easily. Because we now lived in Memphis, church rules dictated we be married in the Richmond Catholic Church, a modern and boring structure. I wanted to be married in Our Lady of Mt. Carmel in Emmett.

The church was a stately, gothic beauty built in the late 1880s. My request and insistence for the church of my choice for the nuptials were frowned upon by the church authorities. After several phone calls to various priests, we were given permission to have the ceremony at the beautiful Gothic structure in Emmett. Lest we get heady with the power of self-will, my request for a particular priest to perform the ceremony was denied. It must be the priest from the Emmett Church, a man I did not know, nor did he remotely know me or Danny. Still, I got my choice of churches. The Emmett Catholic Church was magnificent. The center altar was carved from marble, the pews were ornate carved oak, and stained glass windows surrounded the walls. It made me feel holy.

Danny and I met with the priest, as requested, who informed us we could not be united in marriage at the center altar because Danny was not Catholic. At this point I was still attempting to live the life of a good Catholic girl with the exception of enjoying a full sex life with Danny. I did occasionally confess this sin and then would lament to Danny my guilt, and we would make groundless promises to wait until marriage. However, at the moment my real concern was the center altar issue. I was not going to be married at some insignificant side altar. The priest had a solution. Danny would become Catholic, baptism and all, and would also sign a paper saying that all children born of this union would be reared in the Catholic Church.

"Sure, whatever. I'm marrying you, not a church," was my future husband's reply. In truth, neither one of us had the whisper of real commitment to any religion. Danny's religious upbringing had consisted of absolutely nothing. He grew up thinking that Jesus Christ was a term used to express anger, disgust or even surprise. On the other hand, my upbringing had been Catholic every step of my young life. I was baptized as an infant, acquiring yet another middle name. At birth I was Christine Marie. The church did not find Marie suitable, so Mary was tacked on. Growing up I attended catechism, made my First Holy Communion, for which I got that new dress and a beautiful veil and those horrible baby blue hand-me-down shoes. Next was my confirmation. This did not require a fancy dress, but I did get another name, Cecilia, after a saint. I got slapped by the Bishop. This rite was to signify the suffering of Christ, if I remember correctly. Although I was schooled in religion, understood the rites of passage and followed its forms, my commitment was on the same level as Danny's. This was a means to an end.

Next on the wedding plans agenda was my wedding apparel. Milly and I went to Sperry's Department Store in Port Huron. In 1966 every upscale department store had a wedding department and Sperry's was no exception. This day in most of its detail, had been formulated long ago in my mind so I already knew exactly the dress I wanted. And Sperry's had it for $50. The dress was traditional, white with lace overlay, long lace sleeves, tiny satin buttons down the back, and a big skirt held up with a hoop and ending with a flowing lacey train.

Next I shopped for a veil. Almost immediately I found exactly the head piece and long veil I wanted. It was beautiful and fit on my head perfectly, the shimmering netting hung down my back touching the hem of my gown. It was $100, twice the cost of my dress, but it was magnificent and I loved it.

Then, Milly's voice. "That's a lot of money for a veil," she said. "Do you think you should spend so much on a veil? Will Danny think that's okay?"

There it was, the steel chain being yanked. The little tug. A reminder, delivered with the subtlety of fingernails scrapping across a blackboard. If Milly did not approve, Danny would not. His opinion remained a mirror reflection of his mother's. He was incapable of independent thought inside her universe. And even if by some minute chance he did approve, that would change once Milly spoke of it.

Danny and I had saved money for this once in a lifetime event. We were paying for the entire wedding and honeymoon. No one helped us monetarily or in any other way. But, the implied disapproval was more frightening to me than spending the money on the veil. A veil I would wear once in my lifetime on the most important day of my life. I was still on the precipice of her disapproval and fearful of falling. Instant capitulation followed by total obedience was my only option.

My entire existence up to this point had been learning to silence the person inside me. I had learned that survival meant the ability to, like the science fiction character, become a shape-changer. Antennas perpetually up, mindful of the dangers surrounding me, I became whatever was necessary to survive. And in that moment, it meant smiling and agreeing. It meant stuffing my desires down into the secret chambers of my soul, denying my opinion, and convincing myself that what someone else wanted or thought was right and good was indeed what I desired also. This pattern had begun long before this moment in time. And so, I switched into auto-pilot, became the dutiful, obedient, passive child I had always striven to be. In my mind it had worked in the past, so I saw no point in deviating from a sound pattern of survival. Truthfully, it was anything but sound. It was a side road to my annihilation. And I was on it at breakneck speed.

We, not me, picked out a cheaper veil. Tears stung my eyes, but I smiled and convinced myself I was thrilled. It was one I did not particularly care for but dutifully accepted.

Invitations were ordered, and a bridal shower took place at the house on Boardman Road in Memphis. My trousseau was shopped for and purchased. This I did alone. My mother was conspicuous by her absence, a decision not her own and one for which I was solely responsible. My mother's presence was absent both physically and emotionally. I had shut her out in my desperation to ingratiate myself to Milly and gain her approval. My mother had become merely a guest in all that surrounded the nuptials of her first born daughter who was marrying the son of the woman who had stolen everything she valued and loved. It is difficult to write the words describing that time and impossible to speak them aloud as I consider the pain my selfish actions cost her. She was my mother. My mother.

I had chosen bridesmaids. My maid of honor had been a foregone conclusion since grade school, Pamela. Next, my sister, Shirley Ann, and Teresa, who was not really a choice born of sentiment but more akin to smoking a piece pipe with the enemy. You may not like the tobacco, but you simply did not inhale. Lastly, Ella Morgan, my friend and neighbor from the Emmett time. We had shared a close friendship, and I wanted Ella there with me. Milly once again had a thought, a command really. She decided I must invite Janet to be in my wedding.

At fourteen years old I was a bridesmaid in Janet's wedding. Janet was married at sixteen years old, just weeks before my father and Milly left together to set up housekeeping and my parents' divorce was announced. The timing was convenient for Milly, one less child to bring along as she fled. I have no remembrance of being asked to stand up in Janet's wedding or why I was even considered. Perhaps it was a show of solidarity, blending two families. In truth we were not blended, we were blown apart by a bomb and never restored. Nevertheless, I ended up in a lilac dress with matching shoes and stood as a junior bridesmaid. And now it was my wedding.

"You were in Janet's wedding as a bridesmaid," Milly began. "Did you consider asking her to be in yours?"

"No, I guess not." This I said with all the conviction and authority of a slug burrowing into a tree for safety. The panic of possible disapproval rose up in my chest.

"Well, I thought you might want to consider it. She is in the family." There was the soft voice and steely smile.

"I've already asked Ella," I said.

"Well, I think you need to remember that family comes first. I'm sure Ella will understand."

Family comes first. Was she kidding? But that was that. Ella was out, Janet was in. Janet and I were not even friends. I was angry that yet another decision surrounding my wedding, my day as the bride had been torn from me. And I hated myself for so easily capitulating. It was something that in the years ahead would become second nature to me, so much so that I almost disappeared and lost everything. Almost.

The day arrived. The day, being the twenty-first of May and not the twenty-fifth of June, as originally planned. Weeks previously I discovered that I was pregnant. Not for one brief moment did either Danny or I express sorrow, feel shame or regret over the news. In fact, we both laughed and said how wonderful it was.

179

To have feigned surprise would have been idiotic. Practicing any serious birth control had not been on our agenda. I am not certain either one of us had ever given a thought to the possibility of my conceiving. I was thin and could have certainly hidden the fact of being pregnant for an additional four weeks but could not continue to hide the daily, repeated vomiting. I had morning sickness twelve hours of every day. It did not appear that a flu defense would work, so the wisest option was to move up the wedding date, which we did. This necessitated scaling down our plans. No big reception. No band. No fancy dinner. No one seriously inquired as to why we had suddenly moved our wedding date. We did not offer any explanation. It was 1966 and an out-of-wedlock pregnancy was still kept quiet.

The small house on Boardman was full the morning of the wedding. Almost the entire wedding party was there getting dressed in their finery. It was chaos, but happy chaos. I moved with stealth in and out of rooms, making certain Danny did not catch a glimpse of me before the wedding. In retrospect it seemed ironic, given that I was almost three months pregnant and had already been seen thoroughly by my future husband.

Finally the wedding party arrived at the church. My brother Nicky was there to give me away. Michael, my baby brother, was the ring bearer. The scant number of guests sat in the pews. The music began. Danny was at the altar. His best friend since childhood, Glenn, stood next to him as best man. Danny was the picture of handsome, standing tall, hands folded in front and smiling. I still could not believe that this man was actually marrying me. It was my fairytale come true.

The bridal procession began the walk down the aisle. I liked the long aisle. This would give me the maximum exposure as I walked slowly to the front. Step, pause, step, pause. Shirley Ann, then Teresa, Janet of course, Pamela and then the organ began *Here Comes the Bride*. Nicky put my arm through his, and we started the walk to the altar.

Faces all turned to look at me. No one stood up. Not one person stood to honor the bride as I came down the aisle as tradition dictated. I made the long walk down that lovely church aisle, and every person stayed rooted to their pew. It was a vicious slap to my face, cold water thrown over me. Tears sprang up and threatened to spill over. I blinked them back and stared straight ahead, smiling as always.

"Get up off your asses and stand up for me! I'm the bride. This is my day. I deserve that honor."

I did deserve to be cherished and honored, not just that moment, but before and leading up to my walk down the aisle, a walk I never intended to take again. But I had settled for so little from every one of those people, especially my soon-to-be husband, that this moment was to be no different. And while the thought may have run through my mind to scream those words to everyone seated in the beautiful church, it was nowhere within the realm of possibility that I would do so. No, back then, just eighteen years old, timid, frightened and unsure of myself, I accepted this as one more disappointment to endure. And there was no one in my life to declare otherwise.

What neither Danny nor I knew then, nor could we have imagined, was that our lives would crash and burn during the ensuing years. But, just as the Phoenix of legend, we would eventually rise up, be reborn into lives not just better, but filled with hope and promise.

Our Wedding Day

181

EPILOGUE

We have to wrestle with the lion and the bear on the hills of Bethlehem that we may be prepared to meet Goliath in the valley of Elah.

F.B. Meyer

It is said that you never forget, not really. It is mercy, however, that my mind draws blanks when I try to recall much of my childhood. Snippets such as I have written down do come forth but then the steel door of forgetfulness slams shut and forbids me entrance. I live here now. While at times I feel the foundation of my life is vapor-like, loose and shaking from all that has slipped away and hidden, I know that my real foundation is in my here and now. My husband. My children. My grandchildren. From nothing, Dan and I have built something. From sorrow and cruelty, we have hulled timbers to build a new foundation, one we can look upon as good and right, solid and secure. It is built because we have chosen the good from the evil. It was meant for my harm, as Joseph told his brothers, but God has turned it for my good.

Almost sixty years have passed since the day I lay eyes on Danny Pechacek and his family. Over four decades of those years have been spent being married to him, building a home together and raising a family. And most of those years were spent as strangers living in the same house, pretending we were two people of one mind, with shared goals, working and striving toward a better future for our family. In truth, we spent far too many of our precious years warring against each other, following the lies embedded into us by the four sad, destructive adults known as our parents.

We stood together at an altar and said the words, *I Do*. We pledged to honor and obey, promising to forsake all others and swearing to cleave unto each other. The words were just that, words, empty and spoken in a language we could not hope to comprehend. We, Dan and I, were like two aliens dropped into a foreign land filled with lights and sounds that made no sense. In our efforts to learn and survive, we followed and did the only things we knew to do, imitate parental teaching and follow their role models.

That was a stupid thing to do.

Our parents spent their short lives gasping for air, struggling to survive only to drown in the pools of cruelty and selfishness they themselves helped to create and could not escape. In their desperation to survive, they pulled down seven innocent lives.

Recently Dan and I watched an episode of *Law and Order* in which a mother and father stood facing each other, screaming accusations, shouting blame one to the other while their teenage daughter sat watching and quietly sobbing. In their hatred of each other, the daughter was lost and forgotten.

Dan said to me, "That's our parents. We got lost in their lives. It was all about them, never us."

He was right, of course.

After reading the last of this manuscript, Dan said to me with tears, "We were so young and stupid."

I agreed. And helpless.

Then smiling, he said, "I'd hate to be old and stupid. At least when you're young, you have a fighting chance."

I cannot presume to tell my siblings' story. It is their own to tell. We grew as children within the same walls and called the same two people Mother and Father; but, the sameness ends there. Today, we are sibling, spouse, mother, father, aunt, uncle, and grandparent all doing the best we know to do. Whether or not we are doing a good job will be judged by our legacy, but one thing I know for certain, we are doing a damn sight better than our parents.

PREVIEW FROM

Justice is Good. . .
But Vengeance Will Do

A Story of Grief, Failure and Redemption

Coming in 2013
For More Information go to: www.devotionsbychristine.com

PROLOGUE

The pain was unbearable. Something was wrong, more wrong that I could ever imagine wrong could be.

I lay flat on my back on the narrow bed in the emergency room. Someone told me I would be going into surgery soon. The fire in my chest burned out of control. The monster inside of me pounded away with a thousand searing sledge hammers. The pain did not come in waves, leaving me seconds to gasp a full breath. It was unrelenting in its ferocity.

Exhausted from now eight hours of doing battle with my own body, I wanted to fade into an abyss of sleep. If I could just close my eyes. . . But this ruthless, savage pain tore through me, reminding me that I had lost control of my body hours ago.

Someone sat down on a small stool situated nearest my head. I looked into a stranger's eyes. "I'm your anesthesiologist. I'll be helping you to sleep for surgery," he said, "and I'll be with you throughout." His voice was quiet, unhurried.

His words made little sense to me. I groaned, pushing my torso up with my elbows, trying to get away from this weight of pain that continued to drive and slice its way up and into my shoulders. It was useless. Gurgling, choking sounds came from my throat. My body shook uncontrollably. I was cold and terrified. I did not know if the spasms racking my frame were from the cold or the growing terror at what now seemed my hopeless situation.

The person sitting next to my bed on wheels put a warm hand on my cheek. His soft touch barely registered in my head. The pain screamed, drowning out any incoming touch.

"Why?" The word came out in a strangled sound. Warm tears slid slowly down the sides of my icy temples. My arms seemed paralyzed, unable to raise my hand to wipe away the tears. Every nerve in my body was focused on the pain. "Why would God do this?" I groaned. In answer, or because he had no answer, the man touched my face again.

Two months earlier my doctor had confirmed what we had anticipated. I was pregnant. Danny and I had been trying to get pregnant for four years with no success. Endless tests revealed no obvious problems and no reason why I should not conceive. But finally, now it was true. Our five-year-old daughter, Julie, would have a baby brother or sister. I was both happy and relieved. The months turned into years had convinced me of my failure as a wife and a woman. Frustration often turned to anger. What was wrong with me? Why did my body refuse to do what it was supposed to do? The questions had turned to self-recrimination.

Danny had never said he was unhappy or disappointed, but I sensed something was not right. I was convinced this pregnancy would make whatever it was all good again. Friends congratulated us. Our families were thrilled. But nothing could compare with my own feelings of exaltation.

Then it happened.

Two month into this much anticipated pregnancy, a short eight weeks, it happened. I was sound asleep in a warm bed. It was 2 a.m. Suddenly an explosion went off inside of me. I sat up and grabbed my belly.

"Danny," I shook his shoulder to rouse him up from a sound sleep.

"What?" Half awake, he leaned towards me.

"Something's wrong," I whispered. "Something happened."

"What?" He was waking up fast. "What do you mean?"

"I don't know. My stomach," I was doubled over. "It hurts. I don't know." Panic was beginning to make its way into my voice.

"Are you bleeding," he asked.

"I don't know," my voice was weak, nausea rolling in my stomach and rising up my throat.

"You better check," he said.

I rolled over to put my feet on the floor and felt it; a hot, searing stab. The quick, sharp pain halted my attempt to get out of bed.

"What's wrong?" Danny asked.

"It hurts to move." I stopped and waited.

"Well, okay, go slow," he told me. "Here, let me help you." Danny came to my side of the bed and took my hand.

Slowly inching my way first to sit up and then to slide out of bed, a black wave rolled over me. "I'm going to faint," I whispered. And then everything went black.

Seconds later, I opened my eyes to my husband's face close to mine.

"I'm calling the doctor," he said. After explaining what was happening, I heard Danny say into the phone, "Okay. We'll try that."

"What did he say?" I asked.

"He said you're probably constipated," Danny did not sound convinced. "He said to give you an enema."

I shook my head, not quite comprehending the logic. But anything that helped me stay away from any idea that might suggest trouble with the pregnancy was one I embraced.

For the next several hours we held onto the thought and hope that this pain was a simple fix with a logical explanation.

My husband of just six years prepared to administer an enema on my barely conscious form. I was unable to remain conscious if I even attempted to sit up. Danny held me, his arms locked around my torso, and lead me into the bathroom. I fainted. Seconds later, he tried again. Blackness. Finally, not waiting for me to regain consciousness, he carried me to the bathroom and gently laid me on the floor. The cold tiles on my cheek felt good. Pressure in my chest began to pulse louder. I wanted to stretch, put my shoulders back to make room for whatever was throbbing and building to greater heights in my chest. Every attempt met with new pain and unconsciousness.

Danny sat me up on the toilet seat, put my shoulders back and looked at me. Oblivion hit and I collapsed into his arms. After administering the enema, of which I have no recollection, he carried me back in to our bedroom. His attempts to lay me on the bed brought indescribable pain that, at first made me cry out, and then, faint. Finally he carefully sat me on the bedroom floor, my back resting against the bed. My head down, my chin resting on my chest, I alternated between cries and whimpers. Blacking out became my only respite from the monster inside me.

The awful reality of what was happening was still to come for both of us.

At 8 a.m., after another call to the doctor, Danny, who insisted that my pain was getting worse, not better, was instructed to bring me into the office. In retrospect, it seems ludicrous that we remained blatantly naïve in such a life-threatening situation. But, as had been all our young and now adult lives, we were on our own with no older, wiser heads to guide us.

Unable to stay conscious, which rendered walking on my own out of the question, my husband carried me into the Doctor's office. Within minutes, we were ordered to the nearest emergency room.

I heard the quiet voice again, "They're taking you into surgery very soon," he whispered. "The surgeon will be here shortly."

I forced my eyes to open and look in the direction of the voice. I stared at him, my eyes losing focus as I thrust my head from side to side. My breaths came in gasps, shortened each time by jackhammer thrusts in my chest and shoulders. I panted, each breath coming forth a grunting growl. Blacking out would be mercy, if only for a brief moment. But even that would not come. Instead, new fists of pain came to grab me, cruelly taking me back away from the mercy of unconsciousness.

Two nurses stood over me. One explained she would be starting an IV in my arm. Another gently held my arm as the other probed for a vein. Minutes later and numerous attempts, the IV needle was in and fluids ran into my body.

Left alone, I rolled from side to side, desperate for one brief moment of the agony clawing at my body. Instead, it increased, rising to new heights. Digging into the sheets with my heels, I arched my back, pushing up and away from the razor stabs that now came faster and more violently. I sobbed in full-blown panic.

And then his face. My husband leaned over me, his face just inches from mine. He took my hand in both of his, held it to his chest and then to his face. Danny's face was wet with tears. He did not speak. His eyes followed mine as I thrashed my head back and forth. I slowed my movements and stared into his face.

Two things are seared into my memory of that day. The first is the look on my young husband's face. His handsome features were red and haggard; his eyes, red, clouded with fresh tears he could not hold back. His lips parted slightly as he sucked in a sob. There was fear, real fear on his face that now settled into his beautiful, brown eyes. There was desperation too in the strong shoulders and chest that leaned over and as close to me as he could get. Desperation at how helpless he was to stop this horror; fear, as he came to the realization that his young wife might just die here, today, in this hospital emergency room.

We did not speak. In those brief, insane, agonizing moments, something happened that seared a bond between us. Not spoken, but forged. And like titanium, it resisted any weapon used to sever its circle enclosing us.

The second occurred moments later.

A nurse came and told Danny it was time for my surgery. The pain was now beyond description or endurance. As I was being slowly wheeled away from my husband, I gasped, "It hurts so bad. I can't stand it," I groaned the words. "Can I scream? Is it all right to scream?" I looked at my husband's eyes for reassurance.

His unspilled tears came out in a rush, "Yes," he said between his own sobs. "Yes, you can scream."

And so I did, long, loud, continuous screams. The swinging doors shut behind me. I was in a hallway, my bed up against a wall. I was alone. I kept screaming. No words, just cries and groans. Then a voice. It was mine. "Jesus! I can't do this," loud at first, then quieter, "Do something," I sobbed. "Help me. Please help me," I was crying. "Take this pain. Please."

A hand touched my shoulder. I jerked my head, looking for a nurse or someone standing near me. I was alone. And the pain was gone. It had not eased or lessened. It was gone. I lay staring at the ceiling. The doors to surgery opened and the same gentle voiced anesthesiologist came to me and said, "It's time. They're ready for you."

I was rudely awakened by a man shouting in my face, "CHRISTINE! DO YOU KNOW WHAT DAY THIS IS?"

Shut up, I thought to myself. Still, the voice, "CHRISTINE! DO YOU KNOW WHERE YOU ARE?"

Was he ever going to shut up? "Yes," my voice came slowly up from somewhere dark, a deep, crackling sound.

"WHERE ARE YOU CHRISTINE?"

So loud. Be quiet. "Hospital," I whispered, still traveling back.

"WHY ARE YOU HERE CHRISTINE?"

"Pregnancy. Surgery." The sound of my voice seemed normal, even to me.

"Okay, that's good," this time a gentler sound, softer. "How are you feeling?"

I don't know, I thought, not yet.

He checked the tubes poking out of my arm, scrutinized the bleeping sounds coming from the monitors over my head, and smiled at me. He lifted my hand, turned it over to examine the palm, and studied each finger. "Someone will be in soon to give you a sponge bath."

I lifted my hands close to my face. There was dried blood between each finger, under my fingernails, and streaks trailing up my forearms. The surgeon's first incision had erupted in copious amounts of blood built up inside my chest cavity. And like a hot volcano, it spewed out.

"Your husband is here," he said as he left the room.

Instantly it seemed, Danny came through the door and was at my bedside. We held hands. "There's no more baby," I said.

"I know," he said. "It's okay, it's okay," he squeezed my hand tight. "I love you."

We both cried.

39456039R00125

Made in the USA
Middletown, DE
16 January 2017